Grades K–2

Lessons for Algebraic Thinking

Leyani von Rotz

Marilyn Burns

Lessons for Algebraic Thinking

$$\blacksquare + \blacktriangle = 6$$

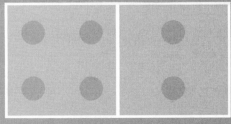

Math Solutions Publications
Sausalito, CA

Math Solutions Publications
A division of
Marilyn Burns Education Associates
150 Gate 5 Road, Suite 101
Sausalito, CA 94965
www.mathsolutions.com

Library of Congress Cataloging-in-Publication Data

Von Rotz, Leyani.
  Lessons for algebraic thinking. Grades K–2 / Leyani von Rotz, Marilyn Burns.
       p. cm — (Lessons for algebraic thinking series)
Includes index.
    ISBN 0-941355-47-0 (alk. paper)
    1. Algebra—Study and teaching (Primary) I. Burns, Marilyn, 1941– II. Title. III. Series.
  QA159 V66 2002
    372.7—dc21
                                        2002010988

Editor: Toby Gordon
Production: Melissa L. Inglis
Cover and interior design: Catherine Hawkes/Cat & Mouse Design
Composition: Argosy Publishing

Printed in the United States of America on acid-free paper
06 05 04   ML   2 3 4 5

A Message from Marilyn Burns

We at Marilyn Burns Education Associates believe that teaching mathematics well calls for increasing our understanding of the math we teach, seeking greater insight into how children learn mathematics, and refining lessons to best promote children's learning. All of our Math Solutions Professional Development publications and inservice courses have been designed to help teachers achieve these goals.

Our publications include a wide range of choices, from books in our new Teaching Arithmetic and Lessons for Algebraic Thinking series to resources that link math and literacy; from books to help teachers understand mathematics more deeply to children's books that help students develop an appreciation for math while learning basic concepts.

Our inservice programs offer five-day courses, one-day workshops, and series of school-year sessions throughout the country, working in partnership with school districts to help implement and sustain long-term improvement in mathematics instruction in all classrooms.

To find a complete listing of our publications and workshops, please visit our Web site at *www.mathsolutions.com*. Or contact us by calling (800) 868-9092 or sending an e-mail to *info@mathsolutions.com*.

We're eager for your feedback and interested in learning about your particular needs. We look forward to hearing from you.

A DIVISION OF MARILYN BURNS EDUCATION ASSOCIATES

To Stefano and Jeffrey

Contents

Introduction

"Who knows what a pattern is?" I asked the first graders at the beginning of the year. The children had spent a good deal of time in kindergarten working with patterns, and many of them had ideas to share.

"It goes on and on," Justin said.

"First you go red and then blue and then red and then blue, like that," Alondra added.

"I can make a pattern," Jazmin said. She clapped her hands twice and patted her head twice, then clapped her hands twice again, and again patted her head twice. As she began to clap her hands again, a few others joined in.

I stopped the children and said, "Yes, that's another example of a pattern. Thank you, Jazmin."

"I think numbers can go in patterns," Graham said, always interested in thinking about numbers.

"Can you give an example?" I asked him.

Graham thought for a minute and then said, "You can count by twos— two, four, six, eight, ten, twelve . . . ," Graham faltered, not certain about the number that came next.

I intervened, "Yes, counting by twos is a good example of a pattern with numbers, and we'll practice that pattern many times this year."

"I can count by tens!" Alvin said proudly. "Can I?"

I nodded "yes" and Alvin counted by tens to one hundred.

Monique slowly raised her hand, with a thoughtful expression on her face. "I think a pattern is something that goes back and forth," she said.

"Can you tell us a little more about your idea?" I asked gently.

"Well," she said, "you can put a triangle, then a square, then a triangle, then a square, and go back and forth like that." Monique's idea was similar to Alondra's, but she was thinking of shapes, not colors.

The children's responses revealed two different ways to think about patterns. Alondra and Monique described repeating patterns. Both of the patterns they suggested were patterns that we could represent as *abab ab . . .* patterns, but there are many variations of these patterns, for example, *aabaabaab . . .*, *aabbaabbaabb . . .* (describing Jazmin's pattern), and so on. Repeating patterns are important for children to investigate, and it's beneficial for children to describe and extend them by listening to and joining in with clapping and snapping rhythms; using a variety of concrete materials; arranging themselves girl, boy, girl, boy; and so on. Repeating patterns are a standard topic in children's early mathematics instruction and are important for encouraging children to look for the order in situations, make conjectures, predict beyond the information at hand, and make generalizations.

The numerical sequences that Graham and Alvin shared, however, are examples of growth patterns. Growth patterns also "go on and on," as Justin said, but the terms in the pattern don't repeat. Instead, they continue on in an orderly way that makes it possible to predict what comes next. Counting books give children experiences with a numerical growth pattern as they help children learn the sequence of the counting numbers. Skip-counting by twos, fives, and tens also provides experience with growth patterns, while also helping develop children's number sense. In the primary grades, it's important for children to have many experiences with growth patterns through experiences that build on explorations with concrete materials, present real-world problems, and rely on imaginary contexts.

As part of children's experiences with growth patterns, it's important not only to focus on sequences, such as counting by ones, twos, fives, or tens, but also to help children see how numbers in a sequence relate to another set of numbers. For example, if we think about the number of wheels on tricycles, we know that on one tricycle there are three wheels, on two tricycles there are six wheels, on three there are nine, and so on. The wheels increase in a growth pattern of threes—3, 6, 9, 12, 15, and so on. But we can relate each of these numbers in the sequence of wheels to a number of tricycles—(1, 3), (2, 6), (3, 9), (4, 12), (5, 15), and so on. In this way, we show the relationship between two varying quantities, the number of tricycles and the corresponding number of wheels. Growth patterns like this one are key to algebraic thinking and form the basis for children's later study of relationships between two variables, which in turn leads to understanding functions. For example, the relationship between tricycles and wheels can be described as $w = 3 \times t$, where the variable w represents the number of wheels and the variable t represents the number of tricycles. (For more mathematical background about functions, see the Appendix.)

Because of the importance of growth patterns to algebraic thinking, the lessons in this book engage children with growth patterns in a variety of ways. While at times we push children in lessons to generalize a growth pattern, we are careful to keep the emphasis of classroom instruction on having the children create, recognize, and extend patterns, talk about what they notice, and, when they're ready, record numerically what they discover. In later grades, children learn to represent patterns algebraically with symbols.

While the lessons in this book address children's algebraic thinking and, in large part, focus on explorations with growth patterns, they also recognize that the main focus of teaching in the primary grades is the development of children's number understanding and skills. Arithmetic is still the time-honored "third R." Examining numerical growth patterns not only builds on the instruction children are already receiving in the area of number and operations but also supports, enhances, and extends children's arithmetic learning.

The concept of *equivalence* is another aspect of algebraic thinking that's key to children's number understanding. For example, it's typical for children in the primary grades faced with adding two numbers, such as 2 + 7, to reverse the order of the addends. They start with the larger number, 7, and count on two more, changing the initial problem to 7 + 2. From many experiences with specific numbers, children see that reversing the order of the addends always produces the same sum. Thus, they develop understanding of the commutative property of addition. Algebraically, we can represent this basic property of numbers using variables: $a + b = b + a$. This representation is a statement of equivalence. The relationship of equality is indicated by the equals sign.

Young children learn about the equals sign early in their study of mathematics, but their learning often results in misconceptions. Typically, children interpret the equals sign as a signal to write the answer. We sometimes hear children read a numerical sentence, $7 + 2 = 9$, for example, as "seven plus two *makes* nine." And we've all seen the errors children typically make in missing-addend problems. For example, in a problem like $3 + \square = 7$, it's typical for children to write, erroneously, a 10 in the box. They see the plus sign and do what they learned, which is to add; they don't think of the equals sign as meaning that what comes before it must be equivalent to what comes after it. Also, while young children will agree that $3 + 4 = 7$ is a true number sentence, they often insist that it's not correct to write $7 = 3 + 4$. And young children typically have difficulty with problems like $2 + 5 = \square + 4$, often adding 2 and 5 and writing 7 in the box. All of these difficulties stem from children's lack of understanding that the equals sign is an indication of equivalence between two quantities. In their early work with numbers, children too often learn to see the equals sign as a signal that the answer comes next.

Some of the lessons in this book are specifically designed to give children experiences that help them develop correct understandings about equivalence. Along with learning about the equals sign, children also learn about inequalities as they explore expressions that are greater than, less than, and unequal to each other. In these lessons, kindergarten children focus on talking about comparing quantities, while first and second graders also get practice with the symbols =, >, <, and ≠.

Variables are another concept key to algebraic thinking. In the example about tricycles and wheels, variables were used to describe the relationship between two quantities: $w = 3 \times t$. In the example about the commutative property of addition, variables were used to represent a general property of mathematics: $a + b = b + a$. In the number sentences $3 + \square = 7$ and $2 + 5 = \square + 4$, the boxes show another way that variables are used in algebra, to represent unknown quantities. However, in this book, the bulk of the experiences focus on growth patterns, equalities, and inequalities. When lessons include variables, we indicate that these experiences are appropriate for second graders and, perhaps, some first graders.

Graphing on a coordinate grid is also an important aspect of algebraic thinking. When describing relationships between quantities, it's important for students to become comfortable with multiple representations, and graphing is one of those representations. Think again about the example of tricycles and wheels. The equation $w = 3 \times t$ is an algebraic representation of the relationship between tricycles and wheels. We can also represent the relationship with a verbal statement: *Tricycles have three wheels, so the number of wheels is equal to three times the number of tricycles*. It's also possible to represent the relationship numerically with pairs of numbers: (0, 0), (1, 3), (2, 6), (3, 9), (4, 12), and so on. Pairs of numbers like these can be displayed in a table called a T-chart. And by plotting points for the pairs of numbers on a T-chart, we produce a graphical representation of the relationship.

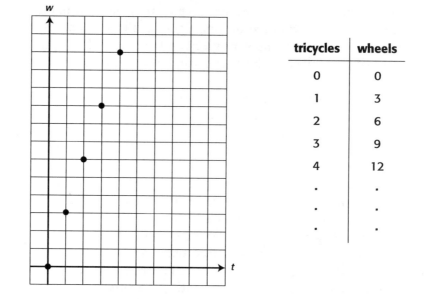

tricycles	wheels
0	0
1	3
2	6
3	9
4	12
.	.
.	.
.	.

In this book, we provide two lessons for teaching and practicing the skill of plotting points and incorporate graphing into one other lesson. As with the lessons that include variables, we indicate that these experiences are appropriate for second graders and, perhaps, some first graders.

Why Algebraic Thinking in Grades K–2?

Teaching algebraic thinking in the elementary grades is a fairly new requirement in the mathematics curriculum. Algebra is no longer relegated to the high school math curriculum, available only to students judged to be capable of learning it. *Principles and Standards for School Mathematics*, published in 2000 by the National Council of Teachers of Mathematics, is the national guide for the mathematics education of students in prekindergarten through grade 12. The first five Standards in the document describe the content goals of the mathematics curriculum. Standard 1, Number and Operations, addresses the mainstay of the elementary mathematics curriculum and the cornerstone of the entire mathematics curriculum in all grades. Standard 2 is Algebra! The message of the document is clear: All students should learn algebra from prekindergarten on up. The document makes the case: "By viewing algebra as a strand in the curriculum from prekindergarten on, teachers can help students build a solid foundation of understanding and experiences as preparation for more-sophisticated work in algebra in the middle grades and high school."

The algebra to be taught to students in the elementary grades should not, however, be a watered-down version of the standard high school course that most of us took. The goal in kindergarten through grade 2 is to develop students' algebraic thinking, building a foundation of understanding and skills while they are young so that they can be successful in their later, more formal study of algebra.

We recognize that some elementary teachers don't feel comfortable with what they remember about algebra. We also believe that teachers can't teach effectively what they don't understand. Therefore, along with presenting classroom-tested lessons, we include a "Background" section for each chapter that addresses the underlying mathematics. In addition, the Appendix, "Mathematical Background," provides explanations about some of the key ideas related to algebraic thinking. Also, the Glossary at the end of the book provides a reference of the algebraic terminology used in the book as well as other terminology that students will encounter later.

The Structure of the Lessons

The sixteen lessons in the book vary in several ways. Some require one class period; others take two, three, or four periods; and many of the lessons are suitable for repeat experiences throughout the year. To help you teach the lessons, each is organized into the following sections:

Overview   This is a nutshell description of the mathematical focus of the lesson and what the students will be doing.

Background   This section addresses the mathematics underlying the lesson and at times provides information about prior experiences or knowledge students need.

Vocabulary   The algebraic terminology used in the lesson is listed alphabetically.

Materials   This section lists the materials needed, along with quantities. Not included are regular classroom supplies such as paper and pencils. Worksheets required are included in the Blackline Masters section at the back of the book.

Time   The number of class periods required is indicated, sometimes with a range allowing for different-length periods and for differences among classes.

The Lesson   This section presents the heart of the lesson with a vignette that describes what occurred when the lesson was taught, providing the details needed for planning and teaching the lesson. Samples of student work are included.

Extensions   This section is included for some of the lessons and offers follow-up suggestions.

We recognize that there are significant differences among kindergarten, first-grade, and second-grade children. Therefore, included in the "Background" section of each lesson are suggestions for using the lesson in each of these grades. We encourage you to take these as general guidelines and, as you do with any instructional materials, make your own decisions about what will be appropriate for the particular students in your class. However, we also identify in the "Background" section the grade level of the particular class described in the vignette. We do this not to discourage you from considering a lesson because your students aren't in the same grade as the students in the vignette, but rather to give you as much information as possible to help you make adjustments to fit your students' needs. You may move more quickly through one section or spend more time on another. As you become more familiar and experienced with these lessons, you'll have a better feel for making appropriate adjustments.

The Content of the Lessons

The lessons are organized into two sections: Part One, "Getting Students Ready," and Part Two, "The Lessons."

Getting Students Ready

The five lessons in this first section require a total of at least eight days of instruction. They introduce students to algebraic thinking and provide students with a foundation of experience on which the rest of the lessons build. Chapter 1, "Caterpillars," introduces students to a growth pattern as they investigate how a caterpillar grows, one year at a time. Chapter 2, "Comparing Handfuls," gives children experience comparing quantities and writing number sentences using the symbols for equal, greater than, and less than. Chapter 3, "Birthday Candles," gives children experience with another growth pattern based on a familiar context—candles on birthday cakes; the students examine the pattern of how the number of candles on a cake increases as they grow older year by year. In Chapter 4, "Dot Cards, Version 1," students get experience decomposing numbers into two addends, comparing quantities, and again recording number sentences, this time using the equals and not equal signs. Chapter 5, "Tic-Tac-Toe: Plotting Points," presents a lesson for teaching students how to plot points on a coordinate grid.

The Lessons

The eleven lessons in Part Two require at least twenty-four days of instruction and build on the experiences in Part One. Three chapters provide students with experience using concrete materials to build and extend growth patterns by representing them on T-charts and describing them in words—Chapter 7, "Pattern Block Fish," Chapter 8, "Worms," and Chapter 12, "Pattern Block Trees." Two chapters draw on real-world problems to give children experience with growth patterns—Chapter 9, "Cows and Chickens," and Chapter 10, "People Patterns." Two other chapters rely on imaginary contexts to help children think about growth patterns—Chapter 6, "Two of Everything," and Chapter 13, "Magic Machines." Three chapters are extensions of Chapters 2, 4, and 5 in the "Getting Students Ready" section. In Chapter 11, "Two Handfuls," students compare the totals of two handfuls and also solve equations with one variable; in Chapter 14, "Dot Cards, Version 2," students extend the experience in "Dot Cards, Version 1" to work with larger numbers; Chapter 16, "Four in a Row," provides a problem-solving experience that helps reinforce the skill of plotting points. In Chapter 15, "Graphing Sums," children combine the various skills they've learned from previous lessons. They write numbers as the sum of two addends, represent the patterns they find on T-charts, and plot pairs of numbers.

Suggestions for Schoolwide Planning

To teach the lessons described in the sixteen chapters requires at least thirty-two days of instruction, plus additional time for extensions and repeat experiences, as suggested for some lessons. To make a schoolwide decision about incorporating algebraic thinking into math instruction for all children, we recommend delegating specific lessons to different grades. However, if you decide to pick and choose lessons on your own, while the sequence of lessons isn't essential, we suggest teaching the ones you choose in the order in which they appear in the book. For example, in Part One, "Getting Students Ready," we present lessons that introduce the big ideas of growth patterns, equality and inequality, and graphing, ordered in the way that makes the best sense to us for introducing children to these concepts.

For kindergarten children, we recommend first teaching Chapters 1, 2, and 3, following the guidelines in the "Background" section for each about teaching the lessons in kindergarten. Chapter 1, "Caterpillars," gives students an initial experience with a growth pattern. Chapter 2, "Comparing Handfuls," is appropriate for giving the children experience with the idea of equality. Chapter 3, "Birthday Candles," gives students an experience with a different numerical growth pattern in a context with which the children are familiar. For additional experiences, we suggest Chapter 6, "Two of Everything," Chapter 7, "Pattern Block Fish," and Chapter 8, "Worms"; these lessons serve to revisit the numerical pattern of Chapter 1, "Caterpillars," in new contexts. Also, we suggest that you do the lesson in Chapter 10, "People Patterns," with only the teacher recording. For each of these lessons, be sure to read the notes about teaching them to kindergarten children. Teaching these lessons will provide kindergarten students with one to two weeks of instruction in algebraic thinking.

Whether or not first graders experienced any of the lessons when they were in kindergarten, we recommend teaching them Chapters 1, 2, 3, and 4 in Part One. Include Chapter 5, "Tic-Tac-Toe: Plotting Points," only if you think learning to plot points is appropriate for your students. After teaching Chapter 1, "Caterpillars," you may want to teach Chapters 7 and 8, "Pattern Block Fish" and "Worms," and push children to see the connections among the three patterns. Except for Chapter 15, "Graphing Sums," and Chapter 16, "Four in a Row," all lessons are appropriate for first graders. However, decide which lessons to incorporate into first grade and which to teach in second grade. We especially recommend for first graders, along with Chapters 1, 2, 3, 4, 7, and 8, to include Chapter 6, "Two of Everything"; Chapter 9, "Cows and Chickens"; and Chapter 10, "People Patterns," without using the 0–99 charts. Teaching these chapters will provide first graders with about two weeks of algebra instruction.

For second graders who haven't experienced any of the lessons previously, start with the lessons in Part One. Then choose from any of the others, as all are appropriate for students in grade 2. While it makes sense to include lessons that first graders in your school haven't experienced, repeat experiences with any of the lessons will benefit the second graders, who can bring an expanded perspective to the explorations. Teaching all of the lessons in the book provides students with about six weeks of algebra instruction. While this may seem like a great deal of time to devote to algebraic thinking, keep in mind that the lessons are extremely valuable for supporting children's number understanding.

In all grades, the lessons recommended don't have to be taught on consecutive days but can be spread throughout the year to support your students' learning of number and operations.

A Final Note

Algebra I students in middle or high school traditionally haven't previously encountered many of the ideas in this book. They are expected to assimilate algebraic concepts and skills in a very short time and often end up with incomplete understandings. Introducing students to algebraic reasoning in the early grades provides a valuable foundation for their later, more formal experiences. For additional background knowledge that can contribute to your understanding of algebraic thinking, please refer to the Appendix.

PART ONE

Getting Students Ready

As stated in the Introduction, the five lessons in this first section require a total of at least eight days of instruction. They introduce students to algebraic thinking and provide students with a foundation of experience on which the rest of the lessons build. Chapter 1, "Caterpillars," introduces students to a growth pattern as they investigate how a caterpillar grows, one year at a time. Chapter 2, "Comparing Handfuls," gives children experience comparing quantities and writing number sentences using the symbols for equal, greater than, and less than. Chapter 3, "Birthday Candles," provides children with experience with another growth pattern based on a familiar context—candles on birthday cakes; the students examine the pattern of how the number of candles on a cake increases as they grow older year by year. In Chapter 4, "Dot Cards, Version 1," students get experience decomposing numbers into two addends, comparing quantities, and again recording number sentences, this time using the equal and not equal signs. Chapter 5, "Tic-Tac-Toe: Plotting Points," presents a lesson for teaching students how to plot points on a coordinate grid.

The "Suggestions for Schoolwide Planning" section in the Introduction offers guidance for choosing and sequencing lessons that are appropriate for your class.

CHAPTER 1

Caterpillars

OVERVIEW

This lesson gives students experience with a growth pattern that involves caterpillars drawn from series of circles. A one-year-old caterpillar has one circle for the head and two more for the body; a two-year-old caterpillar has one circle for the head and three for the body; and the pattern continues in this way. Children explore the pattern by drawing caterpillars, recording on a T-chart, and extending the pattern to figure out how many circles are needed for a ten-year-old caterpillar.

BACKGROUND

Learning to build, extend, and describe growth patterns is an important aspect of developing children's algebraic thinking. Children need no previous experience for this lesson. It's suitable as an introductory activity with a growth pattern. The lesson also introduces for children how to record information about a pattern on a T-chart.

Years Old	Circles
1	3
2	4
3	5
4	6
5	7
.	.
.	.
.	.
10	12

The lesson as described was taught to first graders. For kindergarten children, it's appropriate to present the lesson to the whole class as described in the vignette. Then use your judgment about whether the individual assignment makes sense for your class. You may prefer to continue the exploration as a whole-class activity, taking it as far as makes sense for your students. First and second graders can handle the lesson as described in its entirety.

The pattern of numbers going down in each column is typically easy for young children to identify. Less obvious is the pattern that describes the relationship between the years and the numbers of circles; that is, adding two to the age of a caterpillar gives the number of circles. Point out this relationship with a light touch and keep in mind that many of the students won't see it as useful. For example, later, when children think about how many circles a ten-year-old caterpillar has, most are only comfortable if they fill in the T-chart all the way to 10. Rather than using three dots as shown in the previous illustration, they only feel comfortable if all the numbers are there so that they can focus on what comes next each time.

Years Old	Circles
1	3
2	4
3	5
4	6
5	7
6	8
7	9
8	10
9	11
10	12

I don't worry about this for young children just learning about patterns like this one. They will encounter many more patterns in later grades and will eventually learn not only to use the patterns in the numbers going down the two columns, but also to use the relationships between pairs of numbers to make predictions. Also, in later grades, children will learn to describe the relationship in words; for example: "The number of circles is equal to the number of years plus two." And they will learn to describe it algebraically using symbols for years and circles; for example: $c = y + 2$ or $\triangle = \square + 2$.

VOCABULARY

pattern, T-chart

MATERIALS

- none

TIME

- one class period

I gathered the students on the carpet in front of the board and drew on the board:

"What do you notice about my caterpillar?" I asked the class.

"It's got circles," Braheem commented.

"There's a face," Jared said.

"And a smile," JoAnn added.

"It's got lines for antenna," Elizabeth pointed out.

"How many circles did I draw to make my caterpillar?" I asked. Many hands went up and I asked the students to whisper their answer to someone near them. I heard several students say "two," while others whispered "three." I realized that some students counted only the two circles in the body.

"Let's count the circles together," I said. I pointed as we counted, starting with the head of the caterpillar. Together we counted to three.

"This caterpillar is one year old," I said, writing *1 year old* next to the drawing.

"Now I'm going to draw a two-year-old caterpillar," I said. I made the drawing underneath the one-year-old caterpillar, drawing one circle with a face and antennas and then three circles for the body. Next to the drawing I wrote *2 years old*.

"What do you notice about my new caterpillar?"

"He got bigger. He's eating too much," Elizabeth said.

"He's longer," Ariel said.

"How many circles did I draw to make the two-year-old caterpillar?" I prompted.

The students quietly counted and responded "four," remembering to whisper.

"So the one-year-old caterpillar has three circles and the two-year-old caterpillar has four circles. How many circles do you think I need to draw for a three-year-old caterpillar?" I asked, writing *3 years old* on the board and a question mark where the drawing would go. A few hands went up and others looked puzzled.

"Raise your hand if you think the three-year-old caterpillar is going to be longer than the two-year-old caterpillar," I said. Hands went up.

"They're just eating and eating," Krystal said. I agreed. I erased the question mark and drew a three-year-old caterpillar.

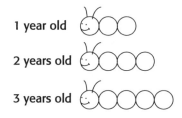

1 year old

2 years old

3 years old

"Raise your hand if that's what you thought the three-year-old would look like," I said. All hands went up. I asked the children to raise hands as a way to give all of them a chance to participate. Even though some children raise a hand when they really aren't sure, I think that they stay engaged and are encouraged to think more about what we're doing.

"So the one-year-old caterpillar has three circles, the two-year-old has four circles, and the three-year-old has five circles," I said to emphasize the pattern, pointing to each drawing as I explained. "How many circles do you think a four-year-old caterpillar will have?"

"Six!" responded several students.

"I agree; it seems to be getting one more circle each year," I commented. "How many circles would a five-year-old caterpillar have?"

"Seven!" came the answer in unison.

"Here's a hard question," I said. "How many circles do you think a ten-year-old caterpillar will have? Think quietly for a moment about this." After a moment, I said to the class, "Now talk with your neighbor about your idea."

When they consider the number of circles for caterpillars in order, it's easy for students to predict what comes next. They think about adding one more circle to the caterpillar from the previous year. It's more difficult for students to see the relationship between the number of years and the number of circles; that is, that the number of circles is two more than the number of years. I ask the question about the number of circles for a ten-year-old caterpillar to encourage children to think about this relationship, but I do so with a light touch, knowing that it's beyond the grasp of many young children.

Some children guessed. Others figured out an answer by imagining the caterpillars, some correctly and others incorrectly.

I then said, "Let's make a T-chart so we have a record just with numbers about how the caterpillar is growing. Then we'll see how the T-chart can help us figure out how many circles the caterpillar will have as it grows older and older." I drew a T-chart on the board next to the caterpillars.

"Let's say together how many circles the one-year-old caterpillar has," I said, pointing to the caterpillar on the board.

"Three," most of the class responded.

On the T-chart I recorded a *1* and a *3*, saying as I did so, "The one-year-old caterpillar has three circles."

1	3

"Who can tell me how many circles the two-year-old caterpillar has?" I then asked.

"Four," came the response.

I wrote the numbers, saying as I did so, "So the two-year-old caterpillar has four circles." I repeated the process for the three-year-old caterpillar.

"Now I need to write something down so I can remember what these numbers are for," I said, pointing to the tops of the columns on the T-chart. "In this column, the one, two, and three stand for one year old, two years old, and three years old, so I'm going to write *Years Old* at the top. On the other side we wrote down three for three circles, four for four circles, and five for five circles, so I'm going to write *Circles* at the top." I labeled the columns of the T-chart.

Years Old	Circles
1	3
2	4
3	5

"It's in order!" Faraaz said enthusiastically. "One, two, three."

"So what would come next in the left column?" I asked the class.

"Four!" I wrote a 4 in the left column.

"And how many circles will a four-year-old caterpillar have?" I asked.

"Six," some students answered.

"Let's see if the numbers on the other side go in order, too," I said, pointing to the numbers listed in the right column as we counted aloud together, "three, four, five."

"What would come next?" I asked.

"Six!" answered the class.

"That matches what we said before. We predicted that the four-year-old caterpillar would have six circles." I wrote a 6 in the right column.

An Individual Assignment   "In a moment you're going to go back to your seats and think about what a five-year-old caterpillar would look like," I said, writing a *5* in the left column of the T-chart and a question mark in the right column.

Years Old	Circles
1	3
2	4
3	5
4	6
5	?

I gave directions: "You'll each have your own paper, but you can talk with the people at your table about what you think. On your paper, you'll draw a five-year-old caterpillar. Also, you'll make a T-chart just like the one on the board, but you'll write a number where I wrote a question mark. There's one more thing to do, and that's to figure out how many circles a *ten*-year-old caterpillar would have." (**Note:** For kindergarten children, use your judgment about whether this individual assignment makes sense. You may prefer to continue the exploration as a whole-class activity, taking it as far as makes sense for your students.)

"That would be a lot!" Ronald commented.

As the students began working, I circulated, observing how they were thinking about and recording the pattern. While hearing several directions at once can be confusing for some children, I give them to provide students with options about how to approach an assignment and to suggest ways the children might begin, not to give a series of steps they are to follow. As I circulated, I gave students nudges and suggestions as needed. I'm careful to avoid trying to help by breaking the task down into little steps, but instead try to keep the children focused on the purpose of the investigation.

Faraaz began by drawing a one-year-old caterpillar. He labeled it *1* and then began his T-chart. He continued drawing caterpillars and adding information to his T-chart until he reached a ten-year-old caterpillar with twelve circles. (See Figure 1–1.)

Veronica also filled in her T-chart down to the ten-year-old caterpillar, increasing the number of circles by one each time. While her paper looked similar to Faraaz's, she worked differently. She began by drawing a T-chart, labeling the columns, and filling in the first pair of numbers. She then drew a one-year-old caterpillar. She recorded the next set of numbers and then drew a two-year-old caterpillar. Continuing in this way, Veronica reached the bottom of her paper after drawing a seven-year-old caterpillar. She turned her paper over and recorded up to a twelve-year-old caterpillar. When she was finished, I suggested she label each of her caterpillars with its age.

Darnell began by making a large T-chart in the center of his paper. He labeled the columns and then wrote the numbers from *1* to *10* in the left column. He ran out of room toward the bottom of the page and his last few numbers were squished together. Darnell was typically very organized and

FIGURE 1–1 Faraaz drew all of the caterpillars from one to ten years old and recorded correctly on the T-chart.

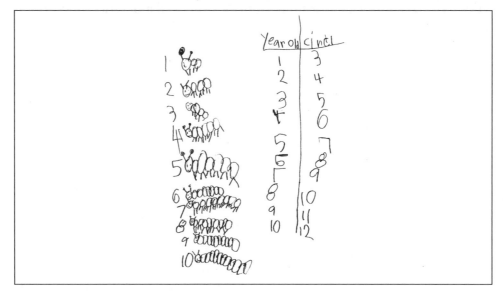

precise, and he wasn't happy with his paper. He erased the numbers and wrote them again, making each number a bit smaller. He then wrote the number of circles for each caterpillar from *3* to *12* by following the sequence of numbers we'd begun together. Finally he began drawing caterpillars, running out of room when he got to the eight-year-old caterpillar.

Dale also began by making a T-chart. He labeled the left column *year* and drew a circle for the label of the right column. He then listed pairs of numbers until he reached the bottom of his paper, recording *16* and *18* on the chart. Unlike Darnell, Dale didn't fill in all of one column and then all of the other, but rather worked out each pair of numbers individually, using the sequence to help him. However, he stopped several times as he worked to check the sequence of each column of numbers. After finishing his T-chart, Dale began drawing the caterpillars. By the end of the period, he'd drawn caterpillars from one to five years old. (See Figure 1–2.)

FIGURE 1–2 Dale only drew caterpillars that were from one to five years old, but he extended his T-chart to a sixteen-year-old caterpillar.

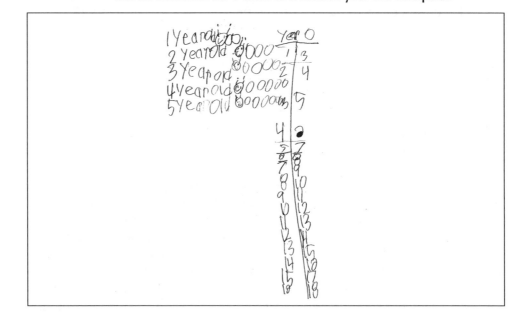

JoAnn began by drawing and labeling a five-year-old caterpillar. She then began listing pairs of numbers. She drew a circle around the second number in each pair to show that it was the number of circles. JoAnn's paper showed the disadvantage of paying attention to the columns of numbers separately, without thinking about the relationship between the ages and the number of circles. JoAnn accidentally skipped writing an 8 in the left column, but she didn't make an error in the right column. Therefore, her chart erroneously indicated that a nine-year-old caterpillar would have ten circles.

Elizabeth also began by drawing a five-year-old caterpillar. She then copied the T-chart from the board, including the question mark. Next she recorded that there were seven circles in the five-year-old caterpillar. Elizabeth then continued by drawing more caterpillars, recording the age and the number of circles after she drew each. (See Figure 1–3.)

Emanuel began by making a large T-chart that covered most of his paper. He filled it in as I had done, carefully referring to the board as he went. He then drew a picture of a five-year-old caterpillar and recorded a 7 next to the question mark on his T-chart. This was a huge accomplishment for Emanuel. (See Figure 1–4.)

When I arrived at Braheem's desk, he had already filled the front of his paper with five caterpillars and had listed their ages. He was working on a six-year-old caterpillar on the back of his paper. I noticed that he'd drawn ten circles for his six-year-old caterpillar. I asked him how many circles he'd drawn and he shrugged his shoulders. I wondered if he was making each new caterpillar longer than the previous one without counting the circles, and I questioned him.

"How many circles does a one-year-old caterpillar have?" I began.

"Three," he confidently answered.

"How about a two-year-old caterpillar?" I continued.

"It's got four," he said quickly. He turned his paper over and showed me the drawings of his caterpillars. I saw that his two-year-old caterpillar had five circles and that both his four- and five-year-old caterpillars had seven

FIGURE 1–3

Elizabeth began by drawing a five-year-old caterpillar, but on her T-chart she included information for caterpillars that were from one to seven years old.

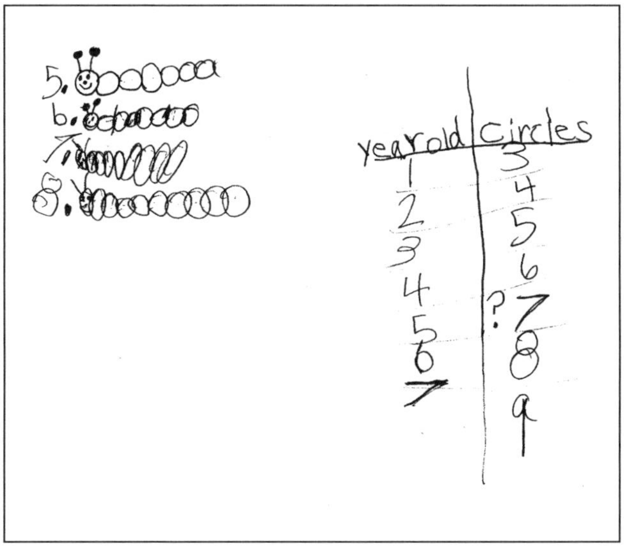

FIGURE 1–4

Emanuel carefully made a T-chart and drew a five-year-old caterpillar.

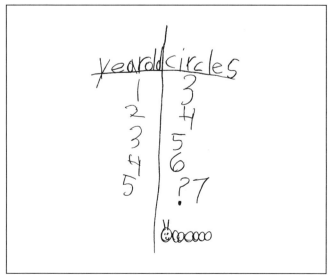

circles. Rather than point this out, I asked him to record the number of circles next to each of his caterpillars. He quickly wrote the numbers *3* through *8* on his six caterpillars, not stopping to count the actual circles he had drawn.

"What caterpillar are you going to draw next?" I asked.

"The seven-year-old," Braheem responded quickly, writing a large *7* on his paper.

"How many circles will it have?" I asked.

Braheem thought for a moment and then said, "Nine." I decided at this time not to say anything to Braheem. I was perplexed that while he seemed to understand the idea of the numerical pattern, he wasn't interested in making accurate drawings. But he was working intently and with confidence, and I decided to leave him to continue and check back a few minutes later.

When I checked back, Braheem had reached the bottom of the paper with a very long ten-year-old caterpillar and a *12* above it. The additional caterpillars he had drawn were labeled correctly, but again his drawings didn't correspond. (See Figure 1–5.) I asked Braheem again how many circles a one-year-old caterpillar had. Again, he answered quickly and correctly.

"Show me your picture of a one-year-old caterpillar," I said. Braheem turned his paper over and pointed to his drawing.

"So a one-year-old caterpillar has three circles," I said to confirm his understanding. He nodded his agreement.

"And the two-year-old?" I asked.

"Four," he answered. I continued asking him for a few more caterpillars.

"Would you check that the caterpillars you drew each have the right number of circles?" I asked. He nodded and began to count. As I watched, I realized that Braheem didn't always count accurately. When his count didn't match the number on his paper, he erased some circles and counted again. Sometimes, however, he didn't touch each circle as he counted. I tried counting with him, holding his hand and touching each circle in the caterpillar. While Braheem demonstrated that he understood how the caterpillars were growing and was able to use the number pattern to predict the next caterpillar in the sequence, he needed more practice counting objects.

FIGURE 1–5 Braheem's numerical recording was correct, even though he didn't draw a T-chart. However, his drawings didn't match his number pattern.

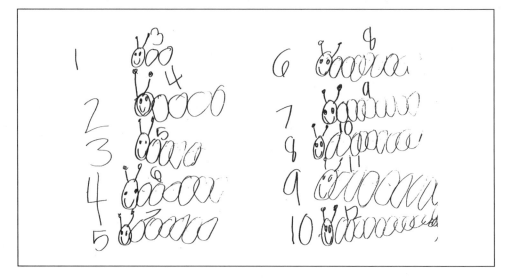

A few minutes before the end of the period, I gathered the children back on the rug and asked them to tell me how to draw a five-year-old caterpillar.

"It's got seven circles and then you make the face at the front," Elizabeth said.

"And it's got antenna," Ariel added. I drew the caterpillar as instructed and erased the question mark from the T-chart.

"Raise your hand if you know how many circles the five-year-old caterpillar has," I said. All hands went up.

"On the count of three, whisper your answer," I instructed, and counted to three.

"Seven!" they whispered. I recorded 7 where the question mark had been and asked who would like to explain how he or she knew it had seven circles.

"Because Elizabeth just told you to make seven," Ronald said matter-of-factly.

"How else could we know that it should have seven circles?" I asked, pushing for more.

"'Cause the numbers go in order," Jared said, pointing to the T-chart.

"Hmm, so after seven circles, what's going to come next?" I asked.

"Eight!" the class answered.

I said, "Let's see if we can fill in our T-chart all the way to a ten-year-old caterpillar. A six-year-old caterpillar has eight circles. A seven-year-old caterpillar has nine circles." I recorded these pairs of numbers and continued, encouraging the children to say the numbers along with me.

When I had recorded that a ten-year-old caterpillar had twelve circles, I said to the class, "I knew that was going to be right even without counting all the way down. I noticed another pattern." I pointed to the first pair of numbers on the chart and said, "I know that to get from one to three, you can add two." I pointed to the next pair of numbers and asked, "What do I add to two to get four?"

"Two," the children answered.

I pointed to the next pair. "Three plus what gives five?" I asked.

"Two," the children answered again. I continued in this way until the children had reported that six plus two gives eight. I then skipped down to the information about the ten-year-old caterpillar on the T-chart.

"We keep adding two to the year to get the number of circles," I said. "I used that pattern for a ten-year-old caterpillar. Ten plus two is twelve, so I knew that the ten-year-old caterpillar had twelve circles."

Together we continued and filled in the T-chart for an eleven- and a twelve-year-old caterpillar before the bell rang for recess. "We have to stop now, but I wonder if we could just keep going and going forever?" I mused. Several students nodded "yes" while others looked at me nervously, as though they thought I might decide to cancel recess.

CHAPTER 2

Comparing Handfuls

OVERVIEW

In this lesson, each student takes a handful of interlocking cubes, counts them, and then snaps the cubes into a tower. In pairs, the students compare their towers and record a number sentence using the symbols for greater than, less than, and equal to. After playing several rounds of the game, students share and discuss their results. The lesson not only gives students experience with comparing numbers, but also helps children learn and practice using the symbols >, <, and =.

BACKGROUND

Learning the meaning of the less than, greater than, and equals sign is important to children's algebraic understanding. In this lesson, the children use these symbols to compare numbers; in a later lesson, they use the symbols to compare sums (see Chapter 11, "Two Handfuls").

For kindergarten children, the emphasis in this lesson should be on comparing the sizes of the towers and using the vocabulary for describing how they compare, not on representing the relationships symbolically. For first and second graders, include the symbolic recording as well. The lesson as described was taught at the beginning of the year to a class of first graders.

It's important that the students have had some experience with the interlocking cubes before teaching this lesson. In this class, the children had previous experience exploring with the cubes and were, therefore, able to focus on the task. If they hadn't, I would have provided time for them to explore with the cubes and satisfy their curiosity.

VOCABULARY

bigger, equal, fewer, greater, less, more, same

- Multilink, Snap, or Unifix cubes, about 12 per student

- *Comparing Handfuls* recording sheet, at least 1 per student (see Blackline Masters)

- 9-by-12-inch white construction paper, 3 sheets

TIME

- one class period, plus additional time for repeat experiences

The Lesson

I gathered the children on the carpet in front of the board and held up a tub of Snap Cubes. I knew that the students had already used Snap Cubes several times in the first month of school, but I wanted to talk about appropriate use of the cubes before giving the directions for the new activity I had planned.

"Today we're going to learn a new activity using Snap Cubes. Who can tell me what you already know about using these cubes?"

"They go together to make towers," Alvin said.

"They're fun to play with," Alondra said.

"We can count them," Graham said.

"You can't throw them," Lauren said.

"You have to share," Manjot said.

I agreed with each of the students' comments and thanked them for remembering how to use the cubes. Then I said, "Now we're ready to learn how to play a new game called *Handfuls*. You play with a partner. Monique and Maurice, will you come up here so we can show the class how to play the game?" They both smiled and came up to the board. I asked Monique to stand beside me on my right so that the class saw her on its left. I asked Maurice to stand on my other side so he was to the class's right.

I explained, "Each of you is going to take one handful of cubes and shake off any extras. Then we're going to compare your handfuls and figure out if Monique has more cubes than Maurice, fewer cubes than Maurice, or the same number of cubes as Maurice. Does anyone have a prediction for how many cubes Monique or Maurice might be able to hold in a handful?"

"I think Monique can hold ten cubes," Graham said.

"I think Maurice can hold twenty cubes because he's bigger," commented Manjot.

"Maybe fifty. Maybe Maurice will take fifty," Joshua added.

I gave all who wanted to predict the chance to do so. Because the students had previously worked with the cubes, even though they hadn't explored counting handfuls of them, my question presented them with a familiar context. This gave me the chance to assess their number sense and see if they could make reasonable guesses. I made a mental note to notice if students' predictions changed over time after they had had experience with handfuls.

"OK, let's find out," I said, motioning to Monique to take a handful of cubes. She dug deep into the bin and took a large handful of cubes. Next Maurice took a handful, stretching his fingers as wide as he could. A few cubes fell off after he picked up his handful, and I reminded the students that they needed to shake their handfuls to get rid of the loose cubes. Monique and Maurice held out their handfuls of cubes to show the class.

"Raise your hand if you think Monique has *more* cubes than Maurice," I said. Many hands went up. "Raise your hand if you think Monique has *fewer* cubes than Maurice," I continued. Many of the same hands went up. "Raise your hand if you think Monique has the *same number* of cubes as Maurice." By now many students were trying to count the number of cubes in each student's hand.

I wasn't concerned about children raising a hand more than once. First of all, their opinion was only a guess, since at this time they didn't have any information about the number of cubes Monique and Maurice had. All options were possible. But, more important, I asked them to respond as a way to encourage them to stay involved and participate. Also, there's no risk to predicting in this way, as no child is being singled out for being right or wrong.

I said, "I notice that many of you are trying to count the number of cubes in Monique's and Maurice's handfuls. If we count the cubes, will it be easier to answer my questions?" Many students nodded.

I turned to Monique. "Monique, let's count your cubes first. I'd like you to snap them together into a tower as we count with you." Monique set her handful of cubes down on the chalk tray, picked them up one at a time, and snapped them together as we counted with her. She had nine cubes.

"Did anyone predict that Monique would have nine cubes in her handful?" I asked the class. Many hands went up, whether they had predicted nine or not.

"I remember that Graham predicted that Monique would have ten cubes in her handful. I think Graham made a good prediction, too. Can anyone tell me why I think Graham's prediction was good?"

"Because ten is more than nine?" Darla offered tentatively.

No other hands went up, so I asked a different question. "If we look at the one to one hundred number chart on the wall, is ten close to nine?" I put a finger on 10 and another finger on 9.

"Yes!" several students said enthusiastically.

"Graham's prediction was very close to the number of cubes in Monique's handful, so that makes it a good prediction," I explained. It's important to help students understand that the goal of estimating is to get close to the actual number rather than guessing exactly. Often students think that any prediction other than the exact number is wrong. Building a sense of what "close" means in estimation is an ongoing process that develops over time. Children need many opportunities to make estimates and discuss the results.

Next, the class counted out loud as Maurice snapped his handful of cubes into a tower. "I've got eight!" Maurice announced proudly. I chose not to discuss the predictions for Maurice's handful because I sensed that I needed to pick up the pace of the lesson.

"You're going to play this game several times, so we need to write something down to help us remember what happened. I'm going to draw two hands on the board, one for Monique and one for Maurice." I drew outlines of two hands on the board and wrote *Monique* above the one on the left and *Maurice* above the other.

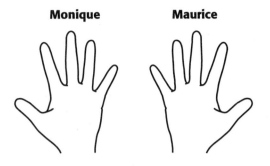

Monique   **Maurice**

"What number should I write in Monique's hand?" I asked.

"Nine!" several students said.

"Why nine?" I asked.

"Because we counted to nine," Simon said.

"Because she has nine cubes," Manuel stated matter-of-factly.

Although it's obvious to some students that it makes sense to write the number nine to represent the cubes in Monique's hand, some students may benefit from the explicit discussion. It's also another opportunity for students to share their thinking and explain things in their own words. I wrote 9 in Monique's hand on the board. I then asked the students what I should write in Maurice's hand, and they agreed that I should write *8*.

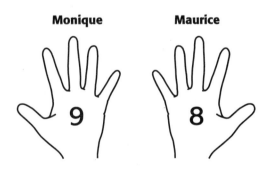

Monique   **Maurice**

"So Monique has nine cubes and Maurice has eight," I announced to the class. I directed Monique and Maurice to stand their towers on the chalkboard tray next to each other so that we could compare them. I made sure that Monique placed hers on the left, so the towers were in the same order as the numbers on the board. I then asked for a show of hands for who thought Monique had fewer cubes than Maurice, more cubes than Maurice, or the same number of cubes as Maurice.

"Turn to someone near you and tell him or her what you think and why," I said. Having students talk to a neighbor gives all of them a chance to share their thinking and gets them accustomed to discussing their ideas with each other. While some children had again raised a hand for each possibility, most knew that Monique had more cubes than Maurice.

"Who would like to tell me what you think and why?" I asked.

"I think Monique has more," Justin offered.

"Why do you think she has more?" I probed. Justin remained quiet, so I added, "I agree with you, Justin, that Monique has more cubes. I'm interested in how you figured that out."

"Because it's more," Justin said, looking a bit uncomfortable. I didn't push Justin further. Oftentimes the first time students are asked to explain what they think they assume that they have made a mistake. Also, students need practice to learn how to explain their reasoning. I thanked Justin for his idea and moved on.

"Who else would like to tell what you think?" I asked.

"Monique's tower has got one sticking up," Lauren said.

"So do you think she has more cubes than Maurice?" I asked to clarify. Lauren nodded.

I then directed the children's attention to what I had recorded on the board. "Let's look at the numbers I wrote in the hands," I said. I pointed to each number as I asked, "Is nine more than eight?"

"Yes!" several students responded.

"Raise your hand if you agree that nine is more than eight," I prompted. All hands went up.

"So now we need to write something down so that we can show what we found out. Here is what mathematicians write to say nine is more than eight," I said and wrote a greater than sign between the two hands. (**Note:** For kindergarten children, it's not necessary to introduce this symbol. Instead, do another example with the children and then have them play in pairs. Ask them to record in some way that makes sense to them so they'll have a record of what happened when they played.)

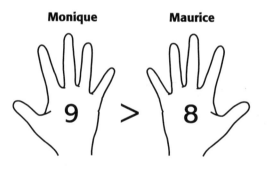

I pointed to the sign and explained, "This sign is a shortcut way to write 'more than.' To me it looks like a little mouth, open wide because it's hungry and wants to eat, and it's trying to eat the amount that is greater." Pointing to the entire expression, I said, "This number sentence says, 'Nine is more than eight.' Or we could say, 'Nine is bigger than eight,' or 'Nine is greater than eight.' Who would like to read the number sentence aloud for us?" Several children volunteered to read the sentence. Some said "more than," others said "bigger than," and Manuel said "greater than."

I posted a sheet of 9-by-12-inch construction paper, wrote the greater than sign, and listed the different words:

>
is more than
is bigger than
is greater than

"You can use the poster to help you when you play the *Handfuls* game with each other," I said. I thanked Monique and Maurice and asked them to sit down.

I showed the children the worksheet I had duplicated.

Comparing Handfuls

"When you and your partner play *Handfuls*, you're going to record on this paper," I said. "You write your name at the top on one side of the paper and your partner writes his or her name at the top on the other side of the paper." I taped the worksheet to the board and modeled this, writing *Monique* on the left side and *Maurice* on the right side. "When you play, you always write the number in your handful in the hand under your name." I recorded *9* and *8* on the worksheet to represent Monique's and Maurice's handfuls and inserted the greater than sign.

The children were eager to get started, but I gave some more directions first. "Before you start playing, I have a few more questions. What if the next time Monique and Maurice play *Handfuls*, Monique has six cubes and Maurice has nine? Then who would have more?" I quickly snapped together the towers and placed them on the chalkboard tray, with Monique's again on the left. Also, I drew two more hands under the other two on the board and wrote *6* in the left hand and *9* in the right hand. I asked the students what they noticed.

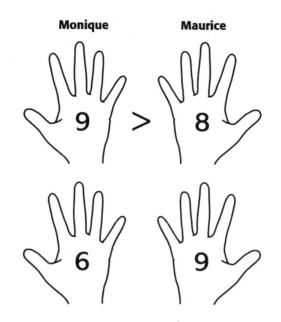

"That one is bigger," Alvin said, pointing to the tower of nine.

"So Maurice has more cubes this time?" I asked. Alvin nodded.

"Does Monique have *more* cubes than Maurice, *less* cubes than Maurice, or the same number as Maurice?" I asked. I knew that grammatically I should ask if Monique had *fewer* cubes than Maurice, but I chose to be ungrammatical to help the children connect the symbol and the vocabulary of "less than." More often children would be comparing two numbers, not two quantities of cubes, and "less than" would then be correct. As the children were learning about the symbol for "less than," I used *fewer* and *less than* interchangeably.

Alondra waved her hand in the air, urgently trying to get my attention. "It's different now. Hers is littler."

"So you agree with Alvin that Monique has fewer cubes than Maurice?" I asked. Alondra nodded.

"Now we need to write something in between the hands to record what we found out," I said and wrote a less than sign.

"This says, 'Six is less than nine.'" I held up the two towers and asked, "Is that true? Is six smaller than nine?" Students nodded in agreement. I pointed to the less than symbol again and said, "This looks like the other symbol we learned, but it's facing the other way. Remember, the mouth wants to eat as much as it can, so it's always open to gobble the bigger number." I posted another sheet of 9-by-12-inch construction paper and wrote on it:

<
is less than
is smaller than

"Let's practice reading what this says," I said, pointing to 6 < 9. "We can say, 'Six is less than nine,' or 'Six is smaller than nine.'" I called on several students to read the sentence aloud.

I recorded this second game on the worksheet I had taped to the board. Then I said to the students, "On your paper, you have three sets of hands so that you can play the game three times. Let's do one more pretend game for Monique and Maurice. What if this time Monique picked up seven cubes in her handful?" I stopped to snap together seven cubes and stand the tower on the chalkboard tray. I continued, "And Maurice picked up seven cubes in his handful, too." I stood another tower of seven cubes next to the first one. "What do you notice?" I asked.

"They're the same!" several students said enthusiastically. I drew two more hands on the board under the other two sets and wrote a 7 in each.

Monique   **Maurice**

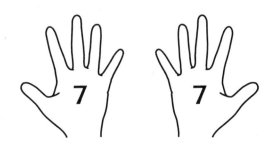

"This time, does Monique have *more* cubes than Maurice, *fewer* cubes than Maurice, or the *same number* of cubes as Maurice?" I asked, pointing to the board.

"The same," the class responded in unison.

"So I need to write something between the hands that tells us that they have an equal number of cubes," I said and wrote an equals sign between the hands.

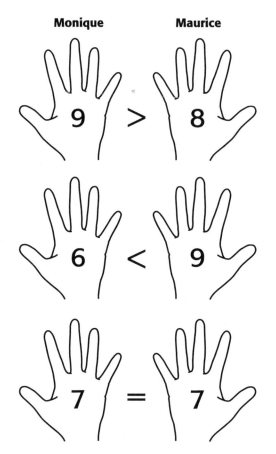

"Here's how we can read this sentence," I said. I pointed to the numbers as I read, "Seven equals seven. Or we could say, 'Seven is the same as seven.'" I posted another sheet of construction paper and recorded:

=
equals
is equal to
is the same as

As I did before, I called on several students to read the expression. Then I also recorded on the worksheet I had posted to show the children what a completed recording sheet would look like.

"Now it's time for you to play *Handfuls*," I said. "When you get your paper, first write your names at the top. Then each of you takes a handful of cubes and shakes off the extras. Snap them into a tower, count them, and write down the number in the hand under your name. Then, together, compare your towers. Remember to write one of these symbols to record what you found out." I pointed to the three posters on the wall. Then I dismissed the students by twos to go back to their seats.

Observing the Students The children quickly got to work writing their names at the top of their recording sheets. Before I put out the bins of Snap Cubes, I made sure that the students had written their names on the same side of the paper as they were sitting to avoid confusion. As I put down the cubes, I pointed out who should take a handful first by pointing to the name at the top left of the page. As students got to work, I circulated, clarifying directions and observing as students counted, compared, and recorded. Many students referred to the posters on the board before writing < or > on their papers. Some also looked at the sample rounds I had recorded for Monique and Maurice.

I walked around the classroom, looking and listening for how students were thinking about counting and comparing numbers.

"Look! I got seven again," Manjot said on the second round of her game with Manuel. (See Figure 2–1.)

"I won again!" I heard Jazmin say. (See Figure 2–2.)

"I got fifteen!" Alvin said as he and Lauren completed the second round of their game. I knew that fifteen were more cubes than would fit into a handful, but I didn't mind because choosing fifteen gave the children experience thinking about larger numbers. (See Figure 2–3.)

I listened to a conversation between Joshua and Sherry. Recorded on their paper was 5 > 6, and Sherry was insisting that Joshua had written the wrong symbol. I offered to read what was on their paper so that they could decide if they wanted to leave it or change it. They agreed. I said, pointing to the poster on the board with > at top, "If I look up at the poster, I see that

FIGURE 2–1

Manjot and Manuel used each of the three signs in their examples.

FIGURE 2–2

Jazmin and Arianna had the same number of cubes only in their first round.

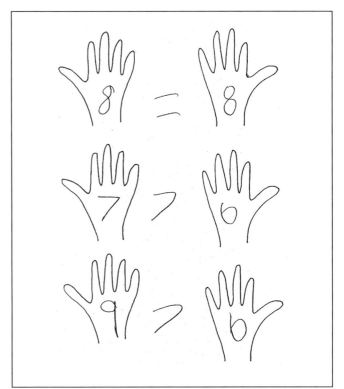

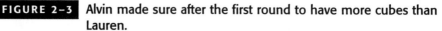

FIGURE 2–3 Alvin made sure after the first round to have more cubes than Lauren.

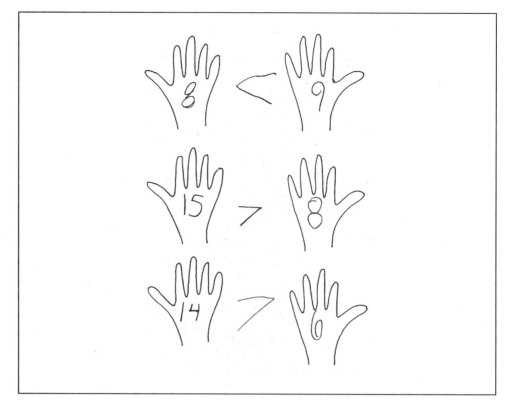

the sign you wrote in between the five and the six means 'more than' or 'bigger than' or 'greater than.' I'll read it the first way, so your paper says, 'Five is more than six.' Is that true? Let's look at your towers." Joshua and Sherry held up their towers side by side.

"But mine is more than hers!" Joshua said.

I responded, "I agree, but look at your paper. Sherry's number is written first, so we start by reading her number. Should it say that five 'is smaller than' six or that five 'is bigger than' six?" I paused, waiting for him to think.

"Smaller," he said.

"Yes, five is smaller than six," I said, pointing to the cubes. "Remember, the mouth has to be open to the bigger number." I pointed to the poster with < at the top. Joshua fixed their paper and they moved on to the next round.

When most of the pairs had had a chance to play three rounds of *Handfuls*, I interrupted the class and gave a warning that we would be stopping very soon. I walked around and took note of a few numbers from the children's papers, choosing a variety that used different signs. After a minute or so, I interrupted the class again and gave directions for cleaning up. When the children had put away the cubes and I had collected their papers, I again gathered the class at the front of the room. "Sit with your partner," I directed.

A Class Discussion   "Raise your hand if you liked playing the *Handfuls* game," I began. All hands were up.

"Raise your hand if you'd like to tell about something you like," I said.

"We got eight equals eight," Jazmin said.

"I got seven every time," Manjot said.

interesting that happened that you might want to share." I walked around and gave each pair of students a paper clip for their dot cards. After cleaning up and collecting all their papers and decks of dot cards, I had the class come to the carpet one last time.

"Who would like to share something interesting that happened?" I asked.

"We got five equals five and four equals four and five doesn't equal four," Alvin said. I fished out his paper and showed how he and Jamila had recorded their answers. (See Figure 4–1.)

Maurice reported next. "We worked all the way down the paper. I always got four and sometimes Manuel got four and it was equal. Sometimes he got five and it wasn't equal." I showed their paper and commented on how different their paper looked from Alvin and Jamila's but how both showed everything they needed to remember. (See Figure 4–2.)

Next I called on Lauren. "We got three and two and three and one," she said. I wrote *3 + 2* and *3 + 1* on the board and asked if they had decided to write the equals sign or the not equal sign in between. Lauren responded, "Not equal, because they both have three and two comes after one."

I then showed the class Lauren and Manjot's paper, which showed this one equation with lots of erased dots under it, and said, to reinforce the more abstract nature of Lauren's explanation, "So sometimes you can figure out the answer just by looking at the numbers."

"Next I'm going to ask you to think about this problem," I continued. I drew on the board two dot cards from an example on Justin and Alondra's paper.

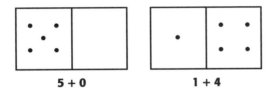

5 + 0   1 + 4

"Should I write an equals sign or a not equal sign?" I asked the class. After giving the children time to think quietly by themselves, I asked them

FIGURE 4–1 Jamila and Alvin had three sets of equal dot cards and two sets of unequal dot cards.

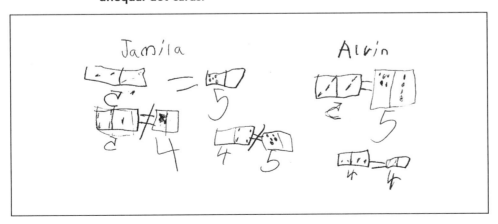

FIGURE 4–2 Maurice and Manuel played ten rounds and, except for omitting one equals sign, recorded correctly each time.

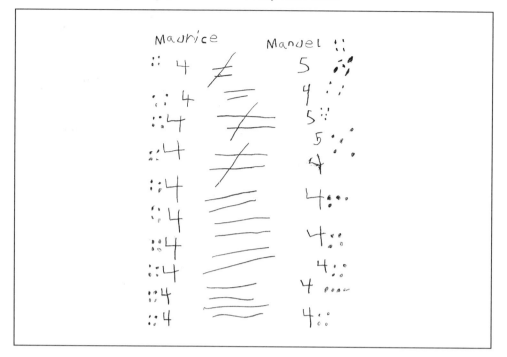

to show a thumb up if they thought equal, a thumb down if they thought not equal, and a sideways thumb if they weren't sure. Most showed a thumb up, but enough showed a thumb down that I felt it was important to talk about the example.

Navi was one of the students who showed his thumb down. I had noticed that on their paper, Navi and Monique, as did a few other children, had used an equals sign only when both cards were identical, when they had both drawn cards that showed five plus zero. They had interpreted the equals sign literally to mean "is exactly the same as," not to mean "is equivalent to." I asked Navi to explain why he thought I should write a not equal sign.

"Because it's different numbers," he said, as though stating the obvious.

"Tell me more about your idea," I said.

"See, it's five and none there and one and four there," he said, pointing to the cards I had drawn on the board.

"I agree that the numbers are different," I said, "but the equals or not equal sign tells if the total number of dots on the first card is the same or not the same as the total number of dots on the second card." I paused a moment and then said, "I wonder how many dots there are on each card? Can anyone help me?" Justin raised his hand.

"That's from my paper," he said, grinning. I fished out his paper, held it up, and invited him to say more. "Look, five plus zero is five," he said, pointing to the first equation on his paper. "And one plus four is five. See, five and five," he said, pointing to the two fives on his paper.

"So since both sides add up to five, you think the cards are equal?" I asked. Justin nodded.

I then turned back to Navi. "How many dots on this card?" I asked him, pointing to the first card I had drawn.

"Five," he answered with confidence.

"And on this one?" I asked, pointing to the other card on the board.

"Five," Navi and several others responded.

"So each card has a total of five dots?" I asked. Navi and a few others nodded in agreement.

I explained, "When both cards have the same number of dots, then the number of dots on the two cards is equal, and you have to write an equals sign. Even if the dots look different or are arranged differently, what's important is how many dots there are altogether on each card." I knew that the class needed many more chances to work with the idea of equality, but for now it was time to go to recess. I made a note to myself to return Navi and Monique's paper to them the next day so that they could look over their examples, count the numbers of dots on the cards they were comparing, and be sure to use an equals sign whenever the numbers were equal. Figure 4–3 shows how one other pair recorded for this activity.

FIGURE 4–3 Sherry and Jermaine's error in the second round was an indication of their confusion. They thought that the unequal sign meant that the numbers were different, not that the sums were different.

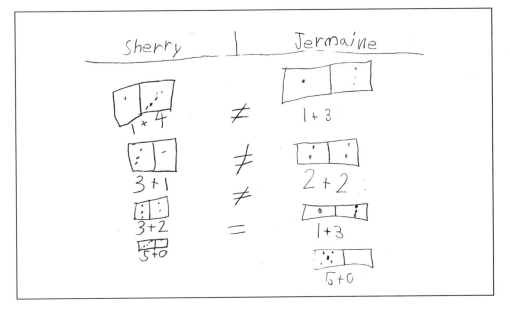

Day 3

The next day, I said to the children, "Today you'll make cards that have six dots and seven dots on each. When you've done this, you'll play the game you played yesterday again, but this time mixing together all of your cards."

The children were now familiar with making cards and the class went smoothly. As children finished their cards, I paired them up so that they could play the game. Each time, I posed a question to suggest a further investigation. I asked, "Do you think you'll write more equals signs or more not equal signs with all these cards together?" Children generally made a prediction but had no reason for doing so. Later I had them count the number of each sign they had used. Figure 4–4 shows how one pair worked on this activity.

FIGURE 4-4 While Joshua drew his dot cards, Simon drew only dots for his first three rounds and then just wrote the number combinations for the last round.

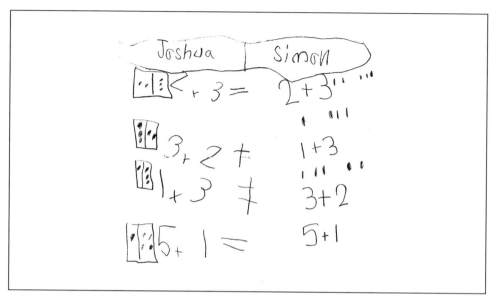

Extensions

1. When children are comfortable with the activity, introduce another version of recording and have them use a greater than or less than sign instead of the not equal sign.

2. For a further extension, introduce the children to Chapter 14, "Dot Cards, Version 2."

CHAPTER 5

Tic-Tac-Toe
Plotting Points

OVERVIEW

In this lesson, students learn to plot points on a coordinate grid by playing a game similar to tic-tac-toe. In this game, however, students mark their Xs and Os on the intersections of lines, not in the spaces as they do with the traditional game. In order to win, they must get four Xs or Os in a row horizontally, vertically, or diagonally. While providing practice with plotting points, the game also encourages students to think strategically.

BACKGROUND

This graphing version of tic-tac-toe engages students' interest, making it an ideal activity for introducing students to plotting points on a coordinate grid. In addition, the lesson is effective for introducing and reinforcing the standard terminology of graphing. The game also promotes strategic thinking, giving a problem-solving aspect to practicing a skill.

    The lesson as described was taught to second graders. We recommend teaching this lesson only in second grade. The procedure is too complicated for many younger children and their time with algebraic thinking is better spent on activities that engage them with patterns and equality.

VOCABULARY

axes, axis, coordinates, diagonal, horizontal, ordered pairs, origin, T-chart, vertical

MATERIALS

- *Tic-Tac-Toe Grid* worksheet (see Blackline Masters)

■ two class periods, as well as additional time for playing

The Lesson

Day 1

Before class I drew a grid low on the chalkboard so the students could reach most of it. To help me do this, I projected an overhead transparency of the *Tic-Tac-Toe Grid* worksheet on the board and traced over the lines. I had considered using the overhead projector to introduce the game, but I didn't because I wanted to have students practice the physical movement of locating points on the graph, and the grid on the board provided a larger scale than a transparency.

After I drew the grid, I marked axes, darkening a horizontal line and a vertical line. At the right end of the horizontal axis, I drew an arrow and a box, and at the top of the vertical axis, I drew an arrow and a triangle. I positioned the axes so that seven was the largest number possible to locate a point that would fit.

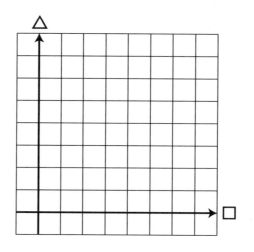

As the children watched me make the grid on the board, they murmured to each other, wondering what we were going to do. Curious about their observations, I asked, "What do you notice?"

"There's lots of squares," Latasha said.

"It has an arrow," Reginald said.

"There are two arrows," Myles interjected.

"A triangle?" Carmen said hesitantly. I agreed with Carmen that there was a triangle.

"And here's a box," I added, pointing to the box I had drawn at the end of the horizontal axis.

I then said, "Today we're going to use this grid for a game board. We're going to play a game similar to one you may know called tic-tac-toe."

"I played that with my brother," Richard said excitedly.

"OK, let's play this version of the game. Who would like to give me two numbers?" I asked. I wanted to show students how to plot points through playing a game rather than explaining all the rules first and then playing.

"Six and eight," Peter suggested.

"Those are good numbers, but they're a little too big for this game. You'll see why in a little while," I said to Peter, wanting to acknowledge his contribution even though the point for his numbers wouldn't fit on the grid.

"Three and two," Bethany suggested.

"Yes, those will work," I responded. "OK, here we go. See where the two dark lines cross? That's where we always start counting." I put my finger on the spot and continued, "I'm going to start there and use Bethany's first number, three, and count three hops toward the box. Then I'll use her second number, two, and count two hops up toward the triangle. Ready? Watch carefully and count with me." I moved my chalk three slow, deliberate hops to the right on the horizontal axis, counting as I went. "What was the second number you told me?" I asked Bethany with the chalk still on the grid.

"Two," she answered.

"We're going to count two hops up, toward the triangle. Ready? Count with me," I said. I counted and moved my chalk up in two distinct moves.

"I'm going to mark an X right here where the two lines cross. This is the point for (three, two)," I said, making a small X on the grid.

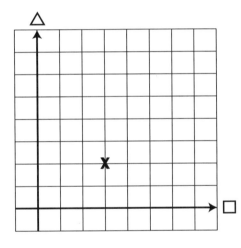

I explained, "The object of this game is to get four Xs or Os in a row. I'll mark Xs for our first game and you'll mark Os. I need to make a T-chart to record the numbers I'm using so I don't forget them." I drew a T-chart on the board and wrote a large *X* above it. The children hadn't seen a T-chart before, but I didn't explain what it was, knowing that they could see how to use it from the context of the activity. "The numbers in the left column will tell you how many hops to go toward the box," I said. I labeled the left column with a box and continued, "The numbers in the right column will tell you how many hops to go toward the triangle." I labeled the right column with a triangle.

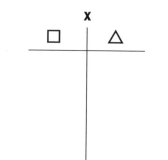

"Bethany helped me with my first move in the game," I said, putting the chalk back on the intersection of the two axes. I wanted to establish the routine for the children that this was the starting place for locating points.

"Her numbers told me to go toward the box, one, two, three," I said, showing the movements again. Hoping to make the connection very explicit between the movements on the grid and the numbers on the T-chart, I added, "So I'll write a three on my T-chart under the box." I recorded a *3* on the chart.

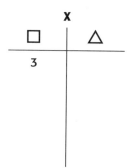

I continued, "Bethany's numbers were three and two. We already used the three, so now we're going to make two hops up, toward the triangle." I moved my chalk as the students counted and landed back on the X I had marked before. "I'm going to write a two on the T-chart on the triangle side," I said. I recorded a *2* on the chart.

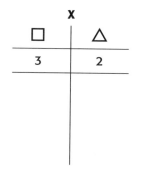

"These two numbers are the directions for how to get to this X," I said, pointing first to the T-chart and then to the X on the grid. "When you play this game, you always have to give the directions in the same order. First you say the number of hops toward the box and then the number of hops toward the triangle," I added, reinforcing this convention for the first of many times.

"By the way," I added in a casual tone, "did I put my X inside a square or did I put my X right on the lines?"

"On the lines!" came a chorus of voices. Children are used to writing Xs and Os in the boxes when they play the traditional game of tic-tac-toe. When plotting points, however, they need to focus on the intersections of the lines. I've learned from experience that placing points in the squares rather than on the intersections of the lines is one of the common mistakes students make when learning to plot points on a coordinate grid. In their later learning, this class would see how using fractions will land points inside squares, but since we were going to be using only whole numbers, this wouldn't occur in our game.

"Now it's your turn to mark an O," I said, addressing the class. "Remember, you are trying to get four Os in a row. Your Os can go in a horizontal line, a vertical line, or on a diagonal." As I said this, I moved my hand in the air from left to right, then up and down, and then diagonally in both directions.

"Think to yourself quietly for a moment about where you think your first O should go," I instructed the class. "Once you decide, figure out what numbers will tell us how to get to that spot." The room was quiet as the students looked intently at the board. Some pointed at the grid and counted silently. In a moment, I asked for a volunteer to come point to the spot where he or she thought the first O should go. I called on Latasha and she came to the board and pointed to a spot on the grid.

"Why did you choose that point?" I asked her.

Latasha responded, "Because it's in the middle." I lightly drew a circle around the point Latasha had indicated.

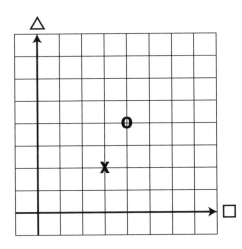

"Now we have to figure out the numbers we need to get there," I said, drawing a second T-chart on the board, labeling the columns with a box and a triangle, and writing a large O above it.

"Let's start at the origin and see how many hops we go toward the box," I said, introducing the new vocabulary by using it in this context. Together the class counted as I moved my chalk four hops to the right until it was directly under the spot Latasha had suggested. "How many was that?" I asked the class.

"Four," the children responded. I told Latasha that she'd better check, and she used her finger to count from the origin just as I had. She agreed it was four hops and I wrote a *4* on the O T-chart in the box column.

"Are we there yet?" I asked, scanning the class to get a sense of whether the students were with me.

"No," came a chorus of voices.

"What's next?" I asked.

"You have to go up," Eugene said.

"OK, count with me," I said. I put my chalk back on the horizontal axis four hops to the right of the origin and then counted up to the spot Latasha had chosen. "One, two, three, four! We made it! I'll mark an O for your team." I darkened the circle to make it a more visible O. Again I asked Latasha to check how many hops up it took. She looked at me, not sure where to begin counting.

"Let's start from the beginning. First we started here where the two dark lines cross at the origin, and we went four hops toward the box," I reminded Latasha as I showed her with my finger. "Then we went from here, up toward the triangle. We counted four hops up to get to the O. Can you count again to check for us?" I left my finger on the horizontal axis, showing her where to start counting up, and she counted the hops, agreeing it was four. I wrote a *4* in the right column of the O T-chart and drew a line to get ready for the next pair of numbers.

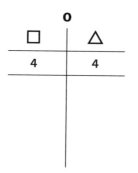

"That's interesting," I observed. "You have the same number on both sides of your T-chart."

"'Cause we went four hops both times," Reginald said in a satisfied voice.

"Now it's my turn again. I'm going to try to make a horizontal row of four," I said in a conspiratorial voice. I lightly drew an X to the right of my first X.

"That's where I want to put my X," I said. "Count with me so I can figure out what numbers to put on my T-chart." Starting again at the origin, I moved my finger first to the right four hops and then up two hops as the class counted with me.

"I think that was four hops toward the box and two hops toward the triangle. Can someone come up and check for us?" I asked. Many eager hands went up. I called on Marlon, who confidently came to the board and confirmed that the point I had indicated was located at (4, 2). I darkened the X and recorded the numbers on my T-chart.

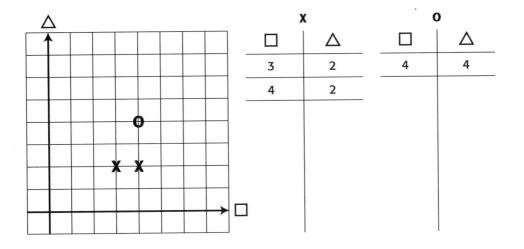

	X			O	
□		△		□	△
3		2		4	4
4		2			

I asked the children to think about the point where they thought their next O should go and to raise a hand when they had an idea. "Since your team is big, you each won't get to pick a point for this game, but soon you'll play just with a partner," I said reassuringly before calling on Nadia.

"I think up there," she said, pointing to a point just out of her reach on the board. I drew a circle to indicate her spot. Again the students counted with me as I showed them how to figure out the coordinates of the point. Nadia repeated my motions, confirming that the point was five hops toward the box and five hops toward the triangle. I marked the O on the grid and recorded the numbers on the O T-chart:

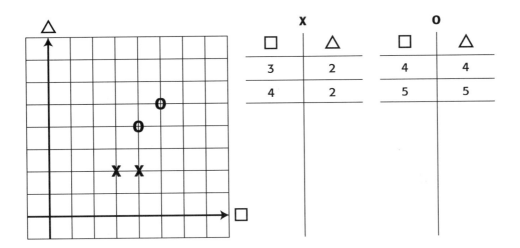

	X			O	
□		△		□	△
3		2		4	4
4		2		5	5

"Why did you choose that point?" I asked Nadia.

She looked at me for a moment and said, "Because it's higher." I asked the class if anyone had another idea of why Nadia's point was a good choice. I wanted to encourage them to think about a strategy for choosing a spot. No one responded, so I gave a hint.

"If we drew a line from Nadia's O to the first O and kept going, could you get four Os in a row and win?" I asked, tracing a diagonal line in the air starting from Nadia's O and going down and to the left.

"It's diagonal!" Lisa whispered.

"Remember you can win with four in a horizontal line, a vertical line, or a diagonal line," I said, writing these three words on the board and drawing lines as a reminder of what the words meant:

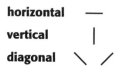

"I've told you my secret strategy," I said. "I'm trying to get four in a row this way," I continued, moving my hand back and forth in a horizontal line over my Xs. "What's this direction called?" I asked, giving the class a chance to practice the new vocabulary.

"Horizontal," a few students said.

"That's right. So if I want to put four Xs in a row horizontally, where should I go next?" I asked. "I know you're not on my team, but maybe you can help me anyway. It's nice to have a partner who helps you even when you're both trying to win." I gave the students a moment to think and then asked for suggestions.

"Hop five toward the box," Peter suggested. I tried his suggestion and paused. "How many should I go toward the triangle?" I asked.

"Two," several voices suggested. I followed their directions and landed on the point just to the right of my previous X. I lightly drew an X.

"That's a good suggestion," I said, pleased that some of the children were connecting numbers to the location of a point on the grid.

"What if I put my X here?" I asked, pointing to the point at (2, 2), which was to the left of my previous Xs. "Would that be a good move, too?" Several students agreed.

"So I have two good choices, point (five, two)," I said, quickly recounting the hops, "or point (two, two)," again quickly locating that point with my finger. I asked for a show of hands to vote for which one they wanted me to use and they overwhelmingly chose their idea. I marked an X at (5, 2) and recorded the coordinates on my T-chart.

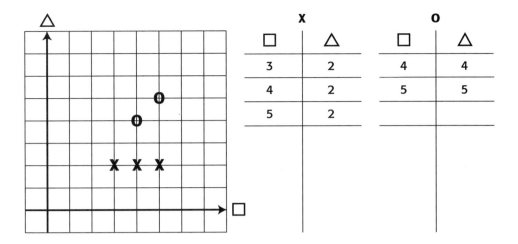

X		O	
□	△	□	△
3	2	4	4
4	2	5	5
5	2		

"It's your turn now and I have a hint for you. You might want to block me because I'm really close to getting four in a row," I said, wanting to introduce the notion of blocking as a strategy. I called on Marie and she came to the board.

"I think we should go here," she said, pointing to the point (2, 2). "I think it's two and two," she said tentatively. Together we checked and confirmed that she was correct. Marie wrote an O on the board for her team and I listed the numbers on their T-chart.

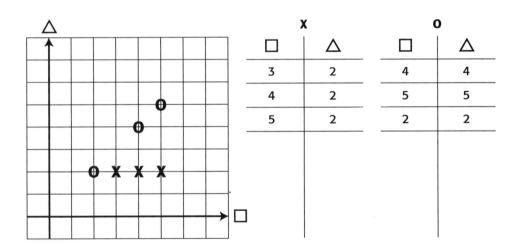

X		O	
□	△	□	△
3	2	4	4
4	2	5	5
5	2	2	2

"OK, you blocked me that way. You only need one more O to have four in a row, but I see what I can do to win," I said, writing the numbers 6 and 2 on my T-chart.

"Where will that be?" I asked the class, pointing to the numbers. After giving them a moment to think, I asked them to raise their hands if they thought that six toward the box and two toward the triangle would make me win. Several hands went up, but many didn't. This was helpful information for me, confirming that the students needed lots more practice before being able to visualize where a point would be from the coordinates.

"Let's try it and see," I said. "Where should I start?" I asked, wanting to review yet again that all counting had to start at the origin.

"There," Myles said, pointing to correct place.

"I agree. That's called the *origin*," I said, writing the word on the board. "It's zero hops toward the box and zero hops toward the triangle." Together we counted to the point *6, 2* and I drew my last X.

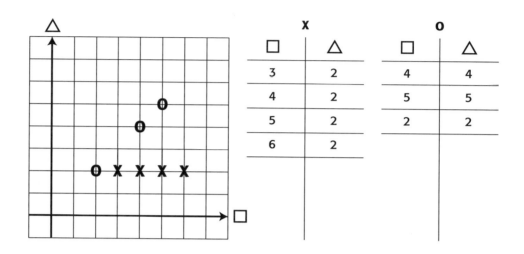

"That's four in a row. But you were really close to getting four in a row, too," I said, putting my finger at (3, 3), which would have been the winning point for them. I thanked the class for being such good sports and asked, "Who would like to play the game again?" Everyone's hand went up and I assured them that we'd play again the next day.

Day 2

I began class the next day by again projecting a grid on the board. "First I'll draw the horizontal lines on the board," I said to reinforce the meaning of *horizontal*. When I had drawn the horizontal lines, I said, "Now I'll draw the vertical lines." When I had completed drawing the grid, I darkened the axes, making sure the lines were more prominent than the other grid lines.

"What else do I need to draw before we play our new kind of tic-tac-toe?" I asked.

"Put the box and the triangle on," Lisa said.

"And the arrows," Jared added.

"Where does the box go?" I asked, curious to see if anyone remembered from the day before.

"On that side," Peter said, pointing to the correct spot at the right end of the horizontal axis. I agreed and drew the box. I asked the class to point to where the triangle went. The students pointed in the correct direction and I added the triangle. Having the children watch as I construct the coordinate grid helps them visualize what the terms *horizontal* and *vertical* mean. Also, it engages children in seeing how a coordinate grid is constructed rather than presenting one to them all completed.

"Today I'm going to have you play in two teams. This half of the class will be the Xs," I said, motioning to the students on the left side of the room. "And this half of the class will be the Os," I added, indicating the students on the right side of the room.

I then explained the procedure we would follow. I said, "When it's your team's turn to play, you can talk to the people near you about where you think your team should go, or you can just think to yourself. Then I'll call on one person from your team to choose a point for your team." A few children began to talk and I called them back to attention.

"Listen carefully," I said and waited until all eyes were on me. "You probably don't all have the same idea for where to move, so somebody else's idea may be different from yours. Also, you may not get to play your idea in this class game. But when this game is over, you'll have the chance to play in pairs and then you'll be able to use your own idea for every move." From past experience I knew that some students get very frustrated in this type of class game, so I reassured them in advance that they would have a chance to play their own game soon.

"OK, Xs," I said, addressing the left side of the room, "you get to go first. Think about where you should make your first move. If you want to, you may talk to the people near you about your ideas." Some students sat quietly while others talked enthusiastically. After a few seconds, I called for their attention and asked who had an idea for where to go first.

"Now, remember, you may not all agree with your teammate, but I'd like you to be respectful of his or her thinking," I said, setting my expectation for their behavior. I called on Travis, who came to the board and put his finger on a point. I lightly marked an X and asked Travis why he chose that spot for his team's first X.

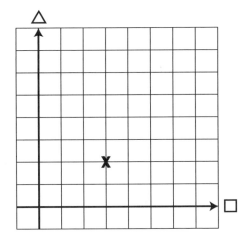

"Cause it's sort of in the middle." Travis replied and then returned to his seat.

"Now let's figure out how to get to that spot," I said, addressing Travis's team members. "We start at the origin, where the two dark lines cross, then first we hop over toward the square, and then we hop up toward the triangle," I said, repeating the directions from the day before and emphasizing the words *over* and *up*. There's no logical reason for first counting over and then up; it's one of the conventions of mathematics that students have to remember. Because of this, I reinforce it as often as I can.

"We always start here at the origin," I said, pointing to the starting place. "Let's count together." I stopped when we had counted three hops over to the right and my chalk was directly under Travis's point.

"Three hops toward the square. Now can anyone tell me how many hops up we need to go?" I asked, wanting to push students to begin counting themselves. After a brief pause, I moved the chalk silently two jumps up to Travis's point. Then I asked the class to tell on the count of three how many hops we went up.

"So to get to Travis's spot, we went three hops toward the box and two hops toward the triangle," I summarized. "We'd better write those numbers down so we don't forget." I drew a T-chart, wrote X on top, labeled the columns with a box and a triangle, and recorded the first set of coordinates.

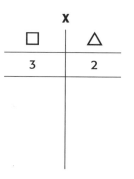

"Now we need to darken the X," I said. "I need someone from the X team to come help me." I called on Lisa, who came to the board and marked the X.

"Let's check and make sure that we wrote the right numbers on the T-chart," I said, pointing to the numbers I had recorded. "The T-chart says to go three toward the box and two toward the triangle."

Lisa put her finger on the origin and counted three hops over and two hops up. "It's right," she said. By going slowly like this, I was giving students a chance to see the connection between the numbers on the T-chart and the points on the grid. I purposely checked the same point several times, hoping to give everyone a chance to understand what we were doing.

I then asked the O team to think about where they wanted to put their first O. After a few moments, I called on Nadia, who came to the board and pointed to a point in the upper right corner of the grid. I lightly drew a circle and asked Nadia why she'd chosen that place for her team's O.

"Because it's bigger," she replied. Together we counted over and up and discovered that Nadia's suggestion was the point (6, 6). I set up a T-chart for the O team and recorded Nadia's point. I called on Myles from the O team to confirm our counting and mark the O. He counted six over and six up, not quite able to touch the board for the last two hops. I offered to draw the O for him and he agreed.

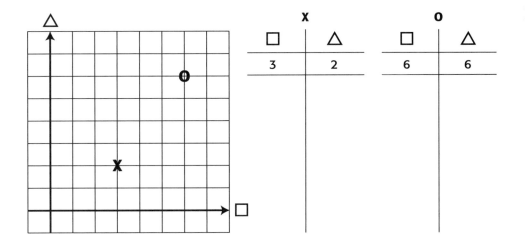

X		O	
□	△	□	△
3	2	6	6

"Now it's the X team's turn again. This time I want you to think about where you want your team's X to go and then I want you to count the hops in each direction. When I call on you, instead of coming to the board and showing me where you want your X to go, I'd like you to tell me the numbers first," I said, wanting to push students to begin figuring out the coordinates themselves. After giving a few seconds for quiet thinking and a few seconds for discussion, I called on Bethany, who said she wanted to put her team's X at point (1, 2) I wrote her numbers on the X T-chart and called on Paulo from the X team to come count and find the right spot for the X. Paulo came to the board, counted, and marked an X for his team. Before moving on, I asked Bethany if the X was where she'd wanted it to be and she nodded "yes."

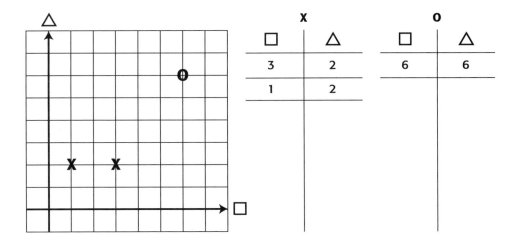

X		O	
□	△	□	△
3	2	6	6
1	2		

Cameron from the O team then chose the point (5, 5). Reginald came to the board, counted, and marked the O. When I asked Cameron why he'd chosen that spot, he replied, "Because we should go diagonal."

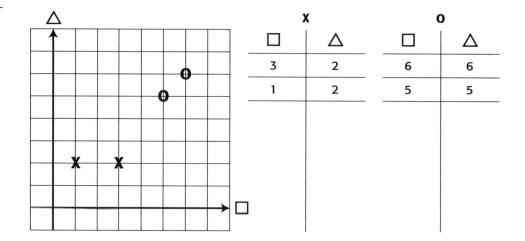

Next, Marlon from the X team chose the point (2, 2). I recorded these coordinates on the T-chart. Avineet came to the board to count. Instead of moving her finger from the origin over one hop, she counted the number one before moving her finger. She did the same when counting up, saying one and not moving her finger until she said two. The result was that she ended up at (1, 1) instead of at (2, 2). This is a common error when children are learning to plot points.

"I'm not sure that's where Marlon wanted to put the X," I said in a puzzled voice, looking at Marlon for his opinion. He shook his head "no" and I continued.

"Put your hand on mine and let's count together," I said to Avineet, crouching down so that the class could see. Avineet put her hand over mine and I very deliberately moved one hop to the right, paused, and said, "One!" I moved one more hop to the right and paused, looking at Avineet. "Two!" she said with a smile.

"Ready? We're going to go up now," I said, looking back at the class to make sure everyone was following us. Again I moved one hop and said, "One!" followed by another hop up, after which Avineet again said, "Two!"

"That's it! Make an X for your team," I directed.

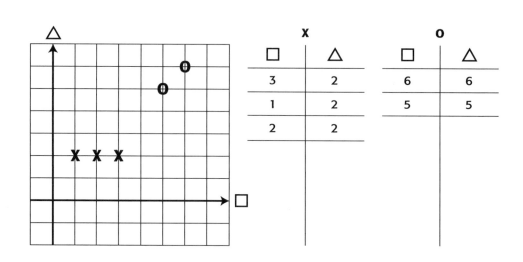

"We've got three in a row!" Marlon commented excitedly. I agreed, pointing out the three Xs in a row. Addressing the O team, I said, "You might want to block the X team because they are close to getting four in a row. Talk to your team about where you could put an O to block the X team." After a few seconds I called for their attention and asked Allison what she thought.

"I know where to go, but I don't know the numbers," she said, sounding a bit distressed.

"We'll help you," I said. "Come up and show us where you think the O should be." Allison came to the board and pointed to the spot to the right of the row of three Xs. I marked it with a light circle.

"Raise your hand if you think Allison picked a good place for your O," I told her team. Many hands went up and I called on Myles to share why he agreed.

"Because we can block them," he said with satisfaction. Together we counted four hops toward the box and two hops toward the triangle. I wrote the numbers on the O T-chart and asked for a volunteer from the O team to come check for us. Marie came to the board, confirmed the point (4, 2), and marked the O for her team.

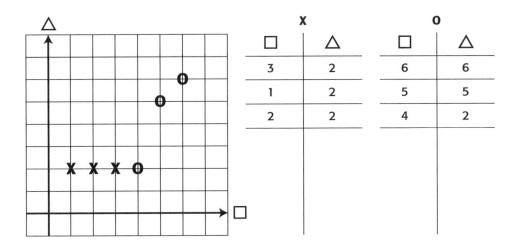

X		O	
□	△	□	△
3	2	6	6
1	2	5	5
2	2	4	2

"It's your turn, Xs," I said, pausing to get all of the students' attention. "Raise your hand if you think you can win with one more X," I said, unsure if they knew that they could put an X at (0, 2). Only a few hands went up and my suspicion was confirmed; many did not realize that they could choose a point directly on an axis. I called on Lisa, whose hand was up, to come show her team where she thought they should put their final X to win the game. She put her finger on the point (0, 2).

"Is that OK?" she asked me. I nodded and lightly marked the point.

Then I turned to her team and said, "Talk to each other about what numbers would tell us how to get to Lisa's spot." After a moment I interrupted. "How many hops is that toward the box?" I asked. I put my finger on the origin and to give a hint, I moved my finger one hop to the right and said, "There's one hop. Is that right?"

"No!" came a chorus of voices. I moved my finger back to the origin and turned to the class with a puzzled look on my face.

"It's no hops that way," Jared said.

"I agree, and what's the number for none?" I asked the class.

"Zero!" came the enthusiastic response.

"So Lisa's point must be zero hops toward the box," I said, writing a *0* on the X T-chart. "And how many hops toward the triangle?"

"Two!" said several voices. I wrote a *2* next to the 0 on the T-chart and demonstrated counting to the point (0, 2).

"And there's where the X team is going to put their fourth X," I said, marking an X on the grid. "Let's all say 'congratulations' to the X team."

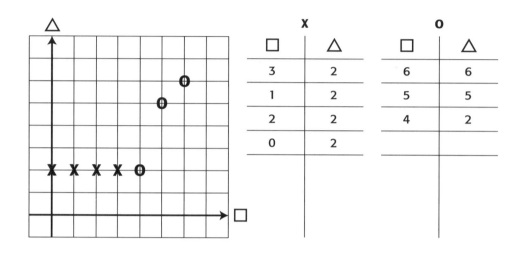

X		O	
□	△	□	△
3	2	6	6
1	2	5	5
2	2	4	2
0	2		

"Now it's your turn to play the game with a partner," I said, holding up a stack of copies of the *Tic-Tac-Toe Grid* worksheets. "Your partner is the person who sits next to you. While I'm handing out the paper for you to play on, you need to decide a few things: who goes first and who is going to be X and who is going to be O. If you go first, it would be nice to let your partner choose which letter to use," I suggested. Before handing a paper to each pair, I confirmed who was going first. If a pair was having trouble deciding, I told them I would come back with a paper when they had come to a decision. This usually sped up the process, as they wanted to start playing the game.

Observing the Students   After a few minutes I interrupted the class and reminded the children to each make a T-chart to record their numbers. As I walked around the room, I noticed that several students were having trouble recording accurately on their T-charts. I remembered that the year before it had taken many students several days to become proficient at matching points on a grid with their coordinates. I knew I had to be patient with the children. Whether or not they were counting accurately, everyone was very engaged in the game.

When I walked past Shivani and Eugene, they told me that they had played an entire game and declared, with huge grins, that they'd both won. I told them that I was glad that they liked the game and that now they needed to record on T-charts the numbers to go with each of their moves. This task took them the rest of the period and Eugene got only two of his points recorded.

I watched Amy and Bethany play a game, resulting in a win for Amy, who managed to have an undisputed six turns to Bethany's four. While tempted to intervene, I held back, wanting to give them a chance to work with the new skill and knowing that sometimes students need practice rather than more explanations.

Marlon and Reginald played a long game in which Reginald began with the largest numbers he could. After getting three Xs in a diagonal line, Marlon blocked him and he started over again on another part of the grid, eventually winning with another diagonal row of four Xs. While not all of the numbers on their T-charts were accurate, their strategies were sound and I decided not to point out their mistakes.

As pairs finished playing, I asked them to write about what happened in their game. Peter wrote: *I did 4 and 4 and 3 and 4 and 2 and 4 and 1 and 4 and thats how I won.* (See Figure 5–1.) Eugene wrote: *I one beciause when I had 3 X and I got one more X I one.* (See Figure 5–2.) Jared wrote about his winning move: *I won becaue I did 8, 3.* His partner, Myles, wrote: *I lost because I had 3 and a row and he is good.*

When the bell rang for recess, several pairs were in the middle of their second game and didn't want to stop. I assured them that they would have a chance to finish their games the next day and they reluctantly went outside.

Over the next few days we played several more rounds of *Tic-Tac-Toe* as a whole class to reinforce the convention of locating points, practice using the new vocabulary, and talk about strategies for playing the game. I also gave the students time to play in pairs. As each day passed, I saw a noticeable improvement in the students' accuracy with identifying the coordinates of points.

FIGURE 5–1

On Peter and Latasha's paper, Peter listed the pairs of numbers he played to describe why he had won. The coordinates on their T-chart correctly match the points on their grid.

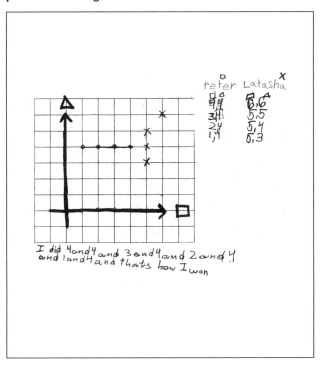

FIGURE 5–2

Eugene and Shivani's T-chart shows that they needed more practice identifying the coordinates for points. They sometimes counted the origin as one instead of zero, a common error when students are first learning.

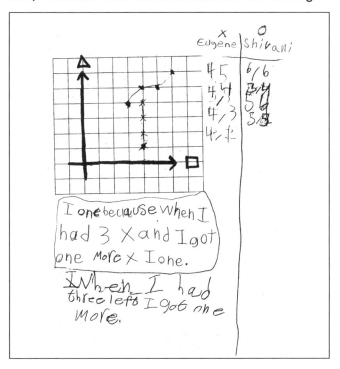

The students' writing also gave me insight into how they were thinking about the game as they get more experience. Lisa wrote about her game with Travis: *I was working realy hard. I see how I can one the game. I think about it all the time even when we are outside.* Marlon wrote: *I won because I went steihtght.* His partner, Latasha, wrote: *I lost because Marlon 5 tord the box and 6 tord the triangle.* Carmen wrote to her partner: *I won because I think and I think away to wen you Richard.* Myles wrote about his partner, Paulo: *I won because he was not looking.* (See Figure 5–3.) The work of another pair is shown in Figure 5–4.

FIGURE 5–3 While Paulo won by marking Xs in a row horizontally, one of the pairs of coordinates he listed on the T-chart was incorrect.

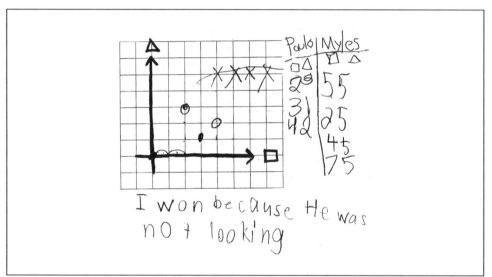

FIGURE 5–4 After children became more experienced, they typically marked more points before someone won the game.

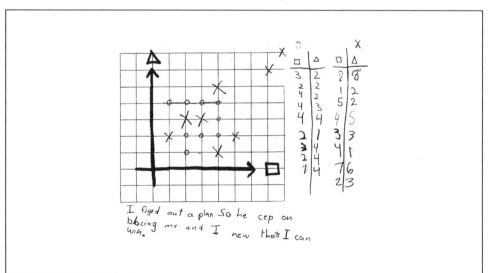

Marie wrote: *I used 4 and 6 and the next number was 3 and 5 the next digits are 2 and 4 and the next digits are 1 and 3. I was thinking about going across. That's how I won. I used a lot of math.* (See Figure 5–5.)

FIGURE 5–5 Navjot and Marie's paper shows that they understood how to record coordinates for points. They each wrote an explanation of what they did.

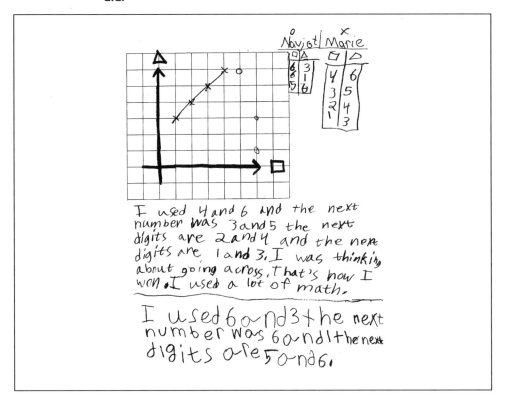

I used 4 and 6 and the next number was 3 and 5 the next digits are 2 and 4 and the next digits are 1 and 3. I was thinking about going across. That's how I won. I used a lot of math.

I used 6 and 3 the next number was 6 and 1 the next digits are 5 and 6.

PART TWO

The Lessons

As stated in the Introduction, the eleven lessons that follow require at least twenty-four days of instruction and build on the experiences in Part One, "Getting Students Ready." Three chapters give students experience using concrete materials to build and extend growth patterns, represent them on T-charts, and describe them in words—Chapter 7, "Pattern Block Fish," Chapter 8, "Worms," and Chapter 12, "Pattern Block Trees." Two chapters draw on real-world problems to give children experience with growth patterns—Chapter 9, "Cows and Chickens," and Chapter 10, "People Patterns." Two other chapters rely on imaginary contexts to help children think about growth patterns—Chapter 6, "Two of Everything," and Chapter 13, "Magic Machines." Three chapters are extensions of Chapters 2, 4, and 5 in Part One. In Chapter 11, "Two Handfuls," students compare the totals of two handfuls and also solve equations with one variable; in Chapter 14, "Dot Cards, Version 2," students extend the experience in "Dot Cards, Version 1" to work with larger numbers; Chapter 16, "Four in a Row," provides a problem-solving experience that helps reinforce the skill of plotting points. In Chapter 15, "Graphing Sums," children combine the various skills they've learned from previous lessons. They write numbers as the sum of two addends, represent the patterns they find on T charts, and plot the pairs of numbers.

The section in the Introduction titled "Suggestions for Schoolwide Planning" offers guidance for choosing and sequencing lessons that are appropriate for your class.

CHAPTER 6

Two of Everything

OVERVIEW

The children's book *Two of Everything*, by Lily Toy Hong, tells the story of a magical brass pot that doubles whatever is put into it. The story is an engaging context for giving students a beginning experience with patterns. Children investigate what happens when their magic pot adds two to what is put in, using cubes to verify the answers, recording on a T-chart, and examining the patterns that emerge. Children next choose a rule of their own, deciding what number the pot will add and recording on a T-chart. They then write a sentence to describe the rule that their magic pot is following.

BACKGROUND

Two of Everything, by Lily Toy Hong, is a Chinese folktale about an elderly couple, Mr. and Mrs. Haktak, who find magic in an ancient brass pot. Mr. Haktak discovers the pot while digging in his garden, and he puts his coin purse into it for safekeeping. When he brings the pot into the house for Mrs. Haktak, she accidentally drops her hairpin into the pot. When she reaches in to get it, she pulls out two hairpins and two coin purses! Mr. and Mrs. Haktak realize their good luck and get to work doubling their possessions. The story takes a hilarious turn when Mrs. Haktak loses her balance and falls into the pot.

This lesson uses the model of the magical pot to introduce students to the idea of functions. A function is a relationship between two variables in which the value of one variable, often called the *output*, depends on the value of the other, often called the *input*. An important characteristic of a function is that for every input, there is exactly one output. For example, if the function rule is to add two to the input number, and the input number is six, then eight is the only possible output number for that input.

In later grades, students study functions in more depth. In grades K–2, however, our goal is introductory and, therefore, we don't identify the activity to the class as an investigation of functions or present a formal definition of *function* to the students. Rather, we keep the focus of the lesson on having students use rules, represent them numerically on a T-chart, write a sentence to describe them, and describe the patterns that result in input and output values.

The lesson as described was taught to a class of first graders and is also appropriate for second graders. With kindergarten children, it's appropriate to teach the lesson up to the point where the first graders were given an individual assignment, focusing the children on the pattern of adding two.

VOCABULARY

pattern, T-chart

MATERIALS

- *Two of Everything*, by Lily Toy Hong (Morton Grove, IL: Albert Whitman & Company, 1993)

- interlocking cubes, at least 10 each of two or three colors per student

TIME

- one class period, plus additional time for extensions

The Lesson

I gathered the students around me on the carpet for our daily ritual of story time after lunch. I showed the cover of *Two of Everything* and read aloud the title and author's name.

"What do you think this story is going to be about? Raise your hand if you have a prediction," I said.

"It's about a grandma and a grandpa," Justin said.

"I think it's about two of everything. Everything is two—two eyes, two ears, two lips, two hands," Manjot commented.

"Yeah, there's two birds and two hills," Graham added, pointing to the cover.

"Let's find out," I said, and began reading the story. I stopped when we reached the page where Mrs. Haktak drops her hairpin into the pot, reaches in to retrieve it, and pulls out two hairpins and also two purses. (Mr. Haktak had put his purse into the pot for safekeeping, and now there were two of those, too!)

"What's going on? What do you think the pot is doing?" I asked.

"They're finding money and stuff inside," Sherry commented.

"They're starting to have two things," Lauren added. I agreed, pointing to the two hairpins and the two purses.

"It said there were five gold coins in each purse. How many coins do you think they have now?" I asked. After pausing for a few seconds to let students think, I asked them to tell someone near them what they thought. After a moment, I called for their attention.

"Raise your hand if you'd like to share what you think," I said, and then added to avoid accusations of stolen ideas, "You can also share what someone near you was thinking."

"I think there's ten because it was five and five," Alvin said. I asked the children to show thumbs up if they agreed with Alvin.

"What if they put those ten coins into one purse and put the purse back into the pot? How many coins would they have then?" I asked. Several hands went up and I asked the students to whisper their answer on the count of three. Most of the voices I heard answered "twenty."

"I agree," I said. "Ten plus ten more is twenty. What if they put all twenty gold coins into one purse and put the purse into the pot again?" After a brief pause, I gave a hint. "What's twenty plus twenty?" I noticed several students checking the doubles chart on the wall before raising their hands. Again I asked them to whisper their answer on the count of three.

"Forty!" came the loud whisper.

I continued reading the story, pausing a few times to allow students to comment. When I finished, I asked students to share what they liked about the story.

"When they both fell in the pot and when they both got together and got their own house," commented Kelvin.

"I like when they got the money," Maurice said.

"I like when he found the purse and when they got two houses," Jamila added.

"I liked the whole book," Manuel said decisively.

A Class Assignment   "Today you'll each think about your own magic pot," I said, drawing a pot on the board. "But instead of having the pot give two of everything, it's going to add one more or two more or three more or maybe even ten more to whatever we put in. See if you can figure out how many my magic pot is adding." I wrote *In* to the left of the pot on the board and *Out* to the right of it. Under In I wrote *1 cube*; under Out I wrote *3 cubes*.

"If you put one cube into the pot, three cubes are going to come out," I explained. To demonstrate, I held up a blue cube and said, "One cube went in." I then picked up two red cubes and held them next to the blue cube. "And three cubes came out," I added. I put the blue cube back in the bin, snapped the two red cubes together, and set them on the chalk tray under the drawing of the magic pot.

"Next I'm going to put two cubes into the magic pot," I said. I wrote *2 cubes* on the board under *1 cube*, took two blue cubes from the bin, and held them to the left of the two red cubes on the chalkboard tray. I said, "The pot is always going to add the same amount, so four cubes come out. Let's check and make sure we now have four." The children joined in as I counted the cubes aloud. I recorded *4 cubes* on the board:

I replaced the two cubes I had put into the pot, again leaving the two red cubes on the chalkboard tray. Pointing to the numbers under the In column, I said, "First I put in one cube and then I put in two cubes. I'll put in three cubes next." I wrote *3 cubes* on the board, took three cubes from the bin, and held them to the left of the two red cubes on the tray.

I then said, "The magic pot is going to add the same number again. Let's count and see how many cubes will come out." We counted the cubes aloud and I recorded *5 cubes*.

"If I follow the pattern, what number should I put into the pot next?" I asked, pointing to the word *In* on the board. Several hands went up. I paused for a moment and then asked the students to count with me as I pointed to the numbers listed.

"One, two, three . . . four!" the class counted. I wrote *4 cubes* on the In list on the board.

"How many cubes do you think will come out?" I asked with a puzzled look on my face. After some quiet thinking time I asked the students to talk to someone near them about what they thought. After a few seconds I asked who would like to share an idea about how many cubes would come out of the magic pot when we put in four cubes.

"I think six," Lauren said, "It's going in order; three, four, five, six." Lauren was looking at the numbers I had listed under Out.

"I think six, too. Four plus two is six," added Nathan, thinking about the rule the pot was following.

"You always add the red ones," Jamila shouted out excitedly.

"And how many red cubes did I always add to the cubes going into the pot?" I asked, picking up the red cubes.

"Two!" the class responded. I recorded *6 cubes* on the board.

"So if I put in five cubes, how many cubes will come out?" I asked, holding up only the two red cubes and returning the others to the bin. After a pause I said, "Count with me from five—five . . . six, seven." I touched the two red cubes as we counted six and seven. I recorded *5 cubes* and *7 cubes* on the board.

"Let's check with cubes," I said. I removed five cubes from the bin and snapped them into a train. Then I added the two red cubes to the train. We counted together to verify that there were seven cubes in all.

"What number is this magic pot always adding?" I asked holding up the two red cubes.

"Two!" the class answered.

"So I'm going to label this magic pot the "Plus Two Pot," I said, writing *+ 2* in the pot.

In		**Out**
1 cube	**+ 2**	3 cubes
2 cubes		4 cubes
3 cubes		5 cubes
4 cubes		6 cubes
5 cubes		7 cubes

"I also want to write a word sentence that tells what the pot is doing. 'The magic pot is adding . . .' Help me finish my sentence," I said, writing as I spoke.

"Two!" answered the class enthusiastically. I finished writing the sentence on the board:

The magic pot is adding 2.

I asked the class to read with me. "The magic pot is adding two," we read in unison.

"Now I want to show you one more thing. These numbers on the board are kind of far apart and it's a little hard for me to keep track of which In number goes with which Out number. I'm going to make a T-chart for the numbers so that they are closer together and I won't get mixed up," I said. I drew a T-chart on the board:

"Why do you think we call this a T-chart?" I asked.

"It's a long skinny T," Jamila said.

"It looks really tall," Alvin added.

"This side will be for the In numbers," I said, labeling the left column *In*. "Help me fill in the numbers." Together we read the numbers from the board and I listed them in the left column of the T-chart. After writing each number, I drew a short horizontal line under the number extending across the T-chart to mark the space for the corresponding number in the right column.

I labeled the right column *Out* and said, "This side will be for the Out numbers. Help me fill in the numbers." Again we read the numbers on the board and I wrote them in the correct spaces on the right side of the T-chart.

In	Out
1	3
2	4
3	5
4	6
5	7

"Now let's check and make sure we wrote the numbers correctly. Our magic pot added how many?" I asked the class.

"Two!" the children answered.

"So the rule the magic pot was following was to add two to whatever I put in," I said and wrote + 2 above the T-chart.

"OK, here we go," I said, pointing to the 1 in the In column. "One plus two is?"

"Three!" the class answered. I moved my finger across to the right column and touched the 3.

"OK, that one works, let's keep going. Two plus two is?"

"Four!" the class answered. Again I moved my finger from the left to the right column. We continued in this way to check the next two pairs of numbers.

"Wow, I bet we could use the patterns to write more numbers on the chart," I said. "Who thinks you know what number I should write next in the In column? Raise a hand when you think you know what number comes next in the pattern." I waited a few moments until most of the children had raised a hand. I called on Maurice.

"You write six," he said.

"Show with your thumb if you agree or disagree," I said to the class. All thumbs were up.

"Why did you say six, Maurice?" I asked.

"They go in order—one, two, three, four, five, six," Maurice replied. I recorded 6 on the T-chart.

"I know what goes next to it," Sherry said.

"What do you think?" I asked.

Sherry answered, "It has to be eight. See, it goes three, four, five, six, seven, and then comes eight." The others showed their agreement and I recorded 8 in the Out column.

+ 2

In	Out
1	3
2	4
3	5
4	6
5	7
6	8

"So you noticed the patterns in the numbers on the chart. Let's check to see if this fits the pot's pattern of adding two. We put six cubes into the pot," I said, stopping to take six cubes from the bin and snap them together into a train. I continued, "Then we added two cubes," I continued, snapping the two red cubes onto the train of six. "Six plus two more is . . . ?" I asked, stopping for the class to answer.

"Eight," the children said.

"Let's count the cubes to check," I said. Together we counted the cubes in the train to verify that there were eight.

An Individual Assignment   "Now it's your turn to make your own magic pot," I announced. "Think to yourself about the number you want your pot to add. That's the rule your pot will follow," I said.

"Two hundred," Alvin suggested.

"You could add two hundred, but that's too big for today. Pick a smaller number," I answered. I wanted the children to use small numbers so that they would have a better chance of being successful with this first assignment. Later, they could repeat the activity with larger numbers.

"Eleven," Nathan suggested.

"Still a little big," I said. "Choose a number that's ten or smaller, and raise a hand once you've made your choice." When all children had raised a hand, I explained what they were to do. "When you go to your table, draw your magic pot and write inside it the number it's adding. Then I want you to think about putting cubes into your magic pot and figure out how many will come out each time. Make a T-chart like the one on the board, and record the number of cubes you put in and the number of cubes that would come out. There are cubes on your tables to help you figure."

Observing the Students   As students started working, I noticed a variety of approaches to the task. Some reached for the cubes first. Others carefully wrote their name on their paper. Most students drew a pot in the middle of their paper and wrote in it the number they were going to add. I noticed that many weren't sure what to do next. I often get the class started on an assignment and then pull them back together for further directions once I see how they are working.

I called for the students' attention and said, "I know you're just getting started, but I'd like to make a suggestion. Make a tower of cubes that shows how many your pot is adding each time," I said, holding up my two red cubes. "If your pot is adding four cubes, make a tower of four. If your pot is adding one cube, make a tower of one. Then when you think about how many cubes are going into your pot, you can use your tower to add the same number each time." I hoped this would help.

The students went back to work. Several took my suggestion and snapped together cubes to match the number written in their pot. After another few minutes I called the class to attention and made a brief announcement reminding students to make a T-chart to record what they were finding out. I circulated, watching and listening as students worked.

Maurice was happily playing with the cubes when I arrived. "It looks like your magic pot is adding ten," I commented, looking at his paper. "How about making a tower of ten cubes?" I suggested.

"OK," he answered, picking up a long stick of cubes, counting to ten, and breaking off the extras.

"What if you put one cube in your pot?" I asked, pulling a single cube from the bin and setting it next to the ten cubes. "How many would come out?"

"Eleven," Maurice answered casually.

"How about making a T-chart and writing that down?" I said. Maurice drew a chart and filled in the numbers *1* and *11*. I sensed that he wasn't going to continue if I walked away, so I said, "What about two cubes?" I put another cube on his paper and waited. Maurice touched the stick of ten and then touched each of the single cubes.

"Twelve," he answered.

"I'd like you to write the numbers on your T-chart and then keep going," I said. Maurice picked up his pencil and I walked away, hoping he would work independently. When I checked back in a few minutes, he'd filled in his T-chart to 4 and 14 and was working on an elaborate construction of cubes. Pointing to his paper, I asked, "What would be next after four?"

"Five," he answered.

"And if you put five in your pot, how many would come out?" I asked, not putting any cubes on his paper.

"Fifteen; I know that one," he answered.

"I'd like you to keep going until you get to ten on the In side," I instructed. Maurice returned to work, I hoped for longer than three minutes this time.

I helped several students get started, having them first use the cubes and then record the numbers on their T-chart. Alvin and Simon both used + 2 for their magic pot but continued past the numbers we'd done together on the board. Alvin tried various In numbers more or less in ascending order. He started with 2, then tried 1, 3, and 4 before recording 7 through 10 in order. I watched as Alvin worked out several pairs of numbers using cubes.

Simon's paper showed that he'd started with 1 in the In column and was continuing in order. He'd labeled his T-chart with the In numbers on the right and the Out numbers on the left. Working from right to left, he carefully figured out each pair of numbers from 1 and 3 to 13 and 15. Simon completely ignored the cubes, quietly counting up two from each new In number to get its Out number.

Juanita used + 3 for her magic pot. It seemed to me that she was working out each combination with cubes and then thinking for a long time before recording a new In number. I noticed that she wasn't choosing the number of cubes to start with in any order, and I asked her how she decided on the numbers. She shrugged her shoulders and said, "I pick a number I can do by thinking."

"So you use the cubes to check?" I asked. She nodded and I left her to her work. Talking with Juanita helped me correct my misconception about how she was working, a reminder of how important it is to talk with children as they work. (See Figure 6–1.)

Darla also used + 3 for her pot. I helped her get started and checked in often, helping her arrange cubes to figure out one plus three, two plus three, three plus three, and so on to seven plus three. Confident that she was OK without more help, I left her to work independently. When I saw her paper toward the end of the period, I noticed that without my assistance she'd added two rather than three to the rest of her In numbers.

Lauren chose + 1 for her pot and filled three long T-charts with her discoveries. She used a wide range of In numbers, including 5, 99, 70, 103, and 10,001. Each time she accurately recorded the sum of her In number plus one. (See Figure 6–2.)

Nathan chose + 10 for his paper and drew a picture for his first set of numbers. To the left of his magic pot he drew one stick figure, and above it he drew ten stick figures.

Graham had a unique approach, imagining putting animals into his magic pot. He started with dogs in a + 2 pot, listing several sets of numbers. When he ran out of room, he asked for another sheet of paper and started a + 3 pot, using cats this time. By the time the period was over, he'd begun a third paper showing pigs and a + 4 pot. (See Figure 6–3.)

FIGURE 6–1

Juanita used + 3 for her magic pot. She didn't choose numbers in any order and checked each Out number by using cubes.

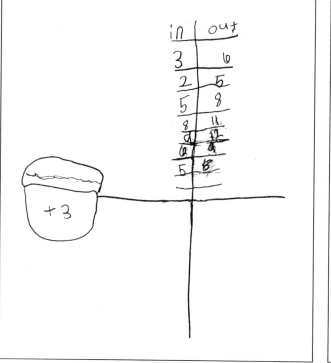

FIGURE 6–2

Lauren chose + 1 for her pot and filled three T-charts using numbers that ranged from 1 to 10,001.

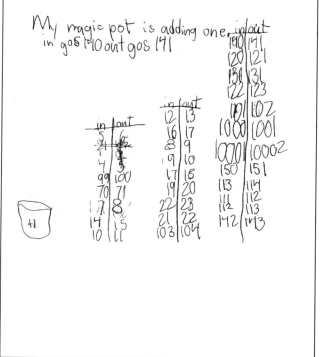

FIGURE 8–3   Peter made a series of drawings. Along with the worm growing from one to four years old, he drew a tree growing out of the ground to a full-grown tree in three years, and then dying in the fourth year. Peter's T-chart has an error showing the number of blocks reversed for the three- and four-year-old worms.

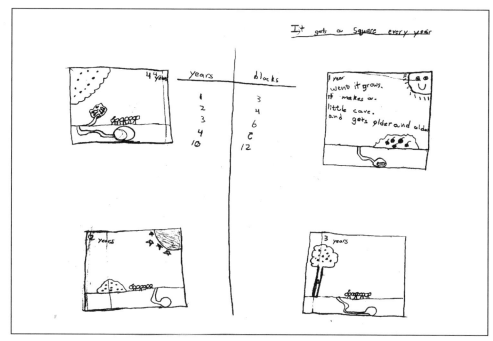

in and it will be 12. The triangles stay the same. The squares keep on adding one every year. Curious to see what she would do, I asked Latasha to think about how to make a hundred-year-old worm. Noticing that Cameron had also finished, I posed the same question to him.

A few minutes before it was time to clean up, I interrupted the students and told them that it was almost time to stop. I noticed Latasha had a distressed look on her face at this news and I went over to her to find out the reason. I saw that in response to my question about a hundred-year-old worm, she was making a very long T-chart. She was close to the end of her paper and had recorded on her T-chart down to a thirty-three-year-old worm with thirty-five blocks.

"You don't have to figure out every worm all the way to one hundred," I said, hoping to help. "If you want you can just tell me about how to make the hundred-year-old worm," I said, unsure if she would be able to do this or not. A look of relief came over her face. She turned her paper over and began writing: *You need 100 squares, and two triangles, for a 100 year old.* (See Figure 8–4.)

I asked for the students' attention and gave directions for cleaning up. Before I excused them for recess, I posed to the entire class the question that I had asked Latasha and Cameron. "I wonder how many blocks it would take to make a hundred-year-old worm?" I asked the students to turn to someone near them to share what they were thinking. I overheard Jared saying to Paulo, "It's one hundred squares and two triangles." Paulo looked back at him in disbelief as the bell rang.

Figure 8–5 shows how another student worked on this activity.

FIGURE 8–4 Latasha drew worms from one to ten years old but then recorded on a T-chart up to a thirty-three-year-old worm, running out of room at the bottom of the page. She then wrote about the number of blocks needed for a hundred-year-old worm.

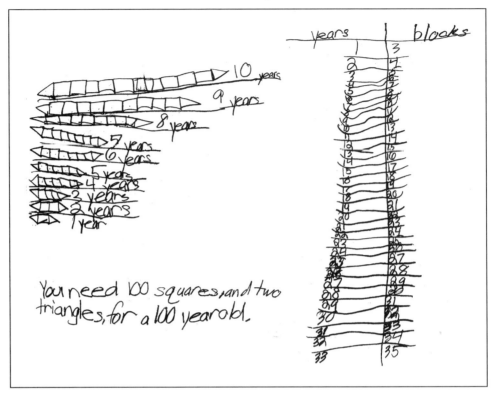

FIGURE 8–5 Lisa accurately drew worms from one to ten years old. When she recorded on her T-chart, she got confused and erased 6, 7, and 8 in the blocks column, replaced them with 8, 9, and 10, and then continued the pattern erroneously.

Cows and Chickens

OVERVIEW

In this lesson, after figuring out how many legs and tails there are altogether on four cows and five chickens, the children investigate the pattern of the number of tails for different numbers of chickens. They record on a T-chart and discuss the patterns they notice. The children next investigate the pattern of the number of legs for different numbers of chickens. They record on a T-chart, look for patterns, and discuss how to extend the pattern. To extend the lesson, children explore patterns for chickens' eyes, beaks, and wings, and then cows' tails, legs, ears, and eyes.

BACKGROUND

The *Cows and Chickens* problem has long been one of our favorites. Suggested in Chapter 2 of *A Collection of Math Lessons, Grades 1–3*, by Marilyn Burns and Bonnie Tank (Sausalito, CA: Math Solutions Publications, 1988), figuring out how many legs and tails there are for a specified number of cows and chickens presents a suitable problem-solving activity for young children. This lesson is an example of how to extend the problem to engage students in algebraic thinking.

The lesson begins by presenting the children with the problem of figuring out how many legs and tails there are altogether on four cows and five chickens. It's important for children to grapple with this problem first so that they understand the context and can then extend their thinking to investigating patterns. The first pattern they consider is the number of tails for different numbers of chickens. While it seems obvious to us that the number of tails is the same as the number of chickens, this isn't obvious to all young children. However, compiling information on a T-chart helps reveal the pattern. Then, thinking about and recording on a T-chart the pattern of legs for different numbers of chickens, the children have an experience with another number pattern, this time with the number of legs being twice the number of chickens. The context of the lesson provides other opportunities to explore patterns as the children consider chickens' eyes, beaks, and wings, and then cows' tails, legs, ears, and eyes.

99

The lesson as described was taught to first graders. For kindergarten children, you may choose to present the initial problem with fewer cows and chickens, perhaps only two cows and three chickens. Then investigate only the patterns of chickens' tails and legs. For first graders, teach the lesson as described, then decide if the extensions are appropriate. The complete lesson with the extensions is appropriate for second graders.

VOCABULARY

pattern, T-chart

MATERIALS

■ pattern blocks

TIME

■ at least three class periods

The Lesson

Day 1

"I have a problem that I'd like you to help me figure out today," I said to begin the lesson. "My problem takes place on a farm. Does anyone know what kinds of animals you might find on a farm?" I gave the children time to think. When many hands were up, to give everyone a chance to share what he or she was thinking, I said, "Whisper your answer to someone sitting near you." I interrupted them after a few moments and said, "Raise your hand if you'd like to tell me the animal you or your partner thought of." As students suggested farm animals, I listed them on the board.

"Horses," Ralonte said.

"A cat," Neha said.

"Cats aren't on a farm!" Jose protested.

"Yes, they are," Precious argued. "They have to eat the mice."

"I know one: cows!" Alex shared.

"And dogs," Damanjit said.

"You know a lot of farm animals," I said, complimenting the class. "Now here's my problem. I was driving by a farm last weekend and I saw some cows and some chickens in a field by the road. The cows were standing and eating grass and the chickens were walking slowly, pecking at the ground. I wasn't going very fast, so I could count that there were four cows and five chickens in the field. But then I wanted to know how many legs and tails they had and it was too late for me to count them. Do you think you could help me figure out how many legs and tails there are for four cows and five chickens?" I asked, ending my story.

The children were eager to tackle my problem. I held up blank paper and a bucket of pattern blocks and said, "You can use pattern blocks, pictures, numbers, and words to help you solve the problem. And you'll have a partner to help you, too. You and your partner will share a paper. Today your partner will be the person who sits next to you at your table."

I then asked the students to remind me about the problem we were working on. "Who remembers how many cows I saw when I was driving?" I asked, curious to see who remembered the details of my story. Many hands went up.

"Lots of you remember," I commented. "I'm going to count to three and I want you to whisper your answer. One, two, three . . . "

"Four!" the majority of the students said in a stage whisper. I wrote on the board:

4 cows

"You're right, I saw four cows. I wrote that down so that we can remember how many there were. I also wrote the word *cows* in case you want to use that on your paper." I pointed to what I had written on the board.

I repeated this process with the number of chickens in my story and added to what I had written on the board:

4 cows
5 chickens

"So now we know how many cows and how many chickens I saw, but what was my big problem that I need your help with?" I asked, wanting to know if the students could restate the problem in their own words.

"You were going too fast so you couldn't count everything," Darleen said.

"That's true," I responded. "What was I trying to count?" I asked, addressing my question to the whole class.

"The feet and the tails!" Sarah said excitedly.

"Chickens don't have feet," Jose retorted, "they have claws. They're sharp."

"That's interesting," I interjected. "Maybe we could say chicken feet can be called claws. You're both right; what I wanted to know was how many legs and tails those cows and chickens had altogether," I said, shifting the conversation back to the problem at hand. On the board I wrote, saying the words aloud as I did so:

How many legs and tails were there altogether?

As I read the question aloud, I reminded the students that they could use pictures, words, numbers, and pattern blocks to work on this problem, then dismissed them to return to their seats.

Observing the Students   As soon as Neha and Precious got their paper, they drew a line down the middle so each would have her own half to work on. I asked them to turn their paper over and think of a way to work together on the same paper. "You make the cows," Precious suggested, as she started drawing a chicken. Neha agreed and started drawing a cow that was a bit smaller than Precious's chicken.

Sarah and Sukhraj also drew lines on their paper, but they explained that the lines were to "keep the animals inside." (See Figure 9–1.)

I checked in with Alex and Patricia. Patricia had a history of difficulty working with a partner, so I wanted to see how things were going. Alex was

FIGURE 9–1 Sukhraj and Sarah shared the work for drawing the cows and chickens. They correctly figured out the number of tails, the number of legs, and the number of tails and legs together.

busily drawing chickens while Patricia was building piles of pattern blocks and then knocking them off the table. I suggested that she work on the paper with Alex and was told by Patricia that Alex wouldn't let her. Alex, on the other hand, maintained that he had offered to share the work and that she hadn't been interested. Having regretted the results of forcing Patricia to work with a partner in the past, I decided to give her a paper of her own. I scooped up the pattern blocks and moved the tub away from Patricia's work area and asked her to draw a picture to go with the problem. I referred to the numbers and words on the board and reminded her that I'd seen four cows and five chickens. I walked away as she painstakingly wrote her name at the top of her paper. I made a mental note to check back with her.

Ralonte and Brandon were each drawing cows and chickens. Brandon had started with cows, while Ralonte had started with chickens. However, they wound up with an extra cow on their paper. They had written the numbers *10* and *29* in the middle of their paper.

"So what do you think?" I asked, curious to hear their explanations of their work.

"See, there's ten legs here on my chickens and that one too," Ralonte said, pointing to the four chickens he'd drawn and the one Brandon had drawn.

"Ah, I see you counted just the chicken legs and wrote that down," I said, interested that Ralonte had created a smaller problem for himself within the context of the larger investigation.

"And it's *29* altogether," Brandon asserted.

"Can you show me how you figured that out?" I asked, wanting to see what Brandon was counting. He began counting the cows' legs and came across a cow with five legs.

"Hey, that's silly," he said, erasing the extra leg.

He counted over again, this time first counting the cows' legs and then counting the chickens' legs, and ended up with twenty-nine legs in all. I noticed that he'd missed counting one of the chicken legs as he went, but I decided not to point this out but instead to give the boys another way to approach the problem.

"Wow, you counted all the legs on the paper. I wonder if you will get the same number if you start by counting the chickens' legs instead of the cows' legs?" I asked. Both boys looked at me with an expression of curiosity and wariness, as though they thought I might be giving them the clue to a magic trick. As I walked away I heard the boys start counting in unison. Rather than stay and be the one to confirm or deny their new count, I hoped that they would discuss their results with each other. From the other side of the room I watched them count and recount the legs on their paper, talking animatedly after each new inventory. However, they never changed what they had written on their paper. (See Figure 9–2.)

After about twenty minutes of work time, I noticed that while everyone was engaged in counting and drawing cows and chickens, few had been able to answer or were interested in my original question. Instead, most students had counted and recorded such things as the number of chicken legs, cow tails, chicken tails, and number of legs altogether. I wasn't sure if they had forgotten my original direction or were simply working their way there by counting smaller groups first. I didn't want students to think that they had made a mistake by counting different sets within the problem I'd posed, so I decided not to interrupt the class to remind them of the original question. However, as pairs of students claimed to be finished without having counted the total number of legs and tails, I clarified the problem and sent them back to their tables to continue working.

After another ten minutes or so, when the period was almost over, I checked back with Patricia. By this time she had managed to state the problem on her paper, writing *4 cows* and *5 chick* and drawing a cow and two chickens. (See Figure 9–3.)

I then called the students to the carpet, collected their papers, and briefly discussed what they had liked about working on the *Cows and Chickens* problem. I asked students to share something their partner had done or said that made them feel good.

Figure 9–4 shows how one pair correctly answered my question.

FIGURE 9–2

Brandon and Ralonte worked diligently but made several errors on their paper. They drew one cow too many and, on one cow, drew an extra leg, which they later erased. They focused their attention on counting all of the legs on the paper, first recording that there were ten legs on the chickens and then, miscounting, that there were twenty-nine legs in all.

FIGURE 9–3

Patricia only managed to get the problem stated on her paper, writing the number of cows and chickens and making a few drawings.

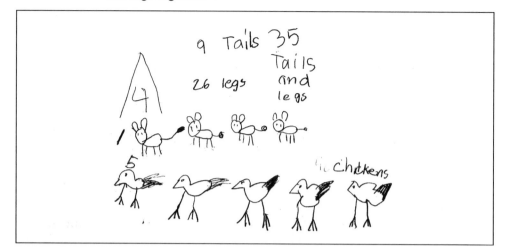

FIGURE 9-4 Priya and Laquinda drew four cows and five chickens and figured out that there were nine tails, twenty-six legs, and thirty-five tails and legs together.

Day 2

The next day I began the lesson by holding up the stack of papers from the day before. "You did a lot of thinking yesterday about my problem with the cows and chickens. Who would like to tell us about what you did?" I was curious to hear what they remembered from the day before.

"We counted nine tails and the legs," Sarah said.

"I did the chicken legs and the cow legs and it was twenty-six," Alex commented.

"We got twenty-six legs, too!" Precious added excitedly.

There were no more hands up, so I asked, "Did anyone else count the tails?" Many hands went up.

"What if we wanted to figure out how many tails there were but we forgot our answer from yesterday?" I asked. "Talk to someone near you about what you think." I wrote on the board:

4 cows
5 chickens

After a few moments I called the class back together. "There's four tails for the cows and five tails for the chickens," Ralonte said slowly, as though he was remembering the numbers as he spoke.

"Me and Sarah got nine from yesterday," Sukhraj said.

"It's nine," Khalia said. "See, five plus four is one, two, three, four, five, six, seven, eight, nine!" Khalia used her fingers, touching each one to her chin as she counted.

"That makes sense to me; how else could we check?" I asked.

"Look at the papers," Alex suggested.

"We could draw a picture," Daria suggested.

I held up several student papers and we counted the tails on the animals. I then drew four cows and five chickens on the board and we counted one more time.

Posing a New Problem   "Now I have a new question," I said. "What if I just wanted to think about one chicken? How many tails does one chicken have?" I was now shifting the children's attention to thinking about the pattern of tails on chickens.

"One!" several students shouted.

"What if I had two chickens? How many tails would there be?"

"Two!" came the answer from the class.

"What if I had three chickens? How many tails would there be?"

"Three!" several eager voices said.

"That's interesting," I said. "I think I hear a pattern. I'm going to write something down so that I can remember what we said." I drew a T-chart on the board and labeled the columns *Chickens* and *Tails*.

Chickens	Tails

"OK, we said for one chicken there's one tail," I said, writing a *1* in the Chickens column and a *1* in the Tails column.

"Then we said for two chickens . . . " I said, pausing as I wrote a *2* under the 1 on the Chickens side of the line—"how many tails do two chickens have?"

"Two!" the class responded again.

"Then how many chickens did I say? One, two . . . ?"

"Then it was three chickens. See, we're counting!" Priya said. I wrote a *3* on the chart under Chickens and paused, ready to write the number of tails. "Ready, whisper!"

"Three!" came the exaggerated stage whisper. I paused and looked at the chart I was creating:

Chickens	Tails
1	1
2	2
3	3

"What do you notice about our chart so far?" I asked the class.

"It's going one, two, three, like Priya said," Daria commented.

"I think it's going in order," Jose said.

"It's the same," Neha said.

"What do you see that's the same?" I asked.

"It's one, one, two, two, three, three," Neha responded, pointing to the numbers next to one another on the chart.

"What if I asked you to figure out how many tails there are for four chickens?" I said without writing anything on the board. Many hands went up. "Whisper to someone near you," I instructed. I heard the children whisper, "Four."

"What about five chickens?" I asked. The students whispered, "Five."

"What about six?" Again they whispered to each other.

"OK, now I have a question I want you to think about and then raise your hand to answer. How many tails would there be if we had ten chickens?"

"Wow!" Jose whispered.

While they were thinking, I filled in the chart for four, five, and six chickens. I then left some room and wrote *10* in the Chickens column and a question mark beside it in the Tails column.

Chickens	Tails
1	1
2	2
3	3
4	4
5	5
6	6
10	?

"I think it's ten tails," Daria said.

"I agree with you, Daria," I said. "Why do you think that there are ten?" I asked.

"Um, cause there's ten?" Daria said uncertainly.

"Who else can help explain why there would be ten tails if we had ten chickens?" I asked the class.

"You can count," Priya said confidently, then counted aloud from one to ten.

"They each have one tail, so I think it's the same number," Alex said.

"Hmm, that's interesting. So if we know that each chicken has one tail, could that help us figure out how many tails there would be for twenty chickens?" I asked to push Alex's idea a bit further.

"Twenty," Alex said confidently. I looked around the room and sensed that some of the students weren't following Alex's reasoning, but I decided to push a little further.

"What about for one hundred chickens? How many tails would there be then?"

"One hundred!" Sarah said excitedly. "It's the same number."

"Wow, that's quite a discovery," I responded. "So for any number of chickens, we can tell how many tails there would be and we wouldn't even have to count!" I was pleased that some of the children had begun to think about mathematical generalizations, but I sensed that the class had been sitting for long enough. Even though it was a shortened math period, I ended the discussion.

Day 3

"Today we're going to think about chickens again," I said, inciting giggles from the class as I drew a chicken on the board. "Yesterday we counted tails. What else do chickens have that we could count?" I asked as I drew a stick figure chicken on the board. Students suggested counting eyes, beaks, legs, wings, feathers, and claws. I listed their suggestions on the board.

"You've thought of a lot of different things to count," I said. "Today let's think about chicken legs." I circled the word *legs* in the list the students had generated. I wanted the children to explore a different number pattern than they had the day before, but also something that they could count. Investigating legs was a logical choice.

"Remember yesterday when we thought about how many tails there would be for one chicken, two chickens, three chickens, and more chickens? Today we're going to think that way again, but this time we're going to count chickens' legs instead of their tails. How many legs are on the chicken I drew on the board?" I asked, wanting to be sure everyone was with me.

"There's two. See, one, two," Priya said, always happy to have an opportunity to count.

"You can just see it's two," Daria commented in a practical tone.

I drew another chicken next to the first one and asked the class how many legs there were for two chickens. Several students answered four legs. We counted to confirm the answer and I drew a third chicken on the board. Some put hands up immediately, while others silently counted the legs on the board. I couldn't tell if the rest of the students were thinking or were confused.

"Whisper what you think and why to someone near you," I instructed, wanting to give everyone a chance to speak before we discussed the answer. I also wanted the students who may not have had a way to think about this problem to hear another student's thinking.

"Before you share your answers, I think I should write something down so that we can remember what we've said so far," I said. "Remember the T-chart I made yesterday with chickens and tails?" I drew a T-chart on the board and explained, "We're still talking about chickens, so I'm going to write 'Chickens' here." I wrote *Chickens* at the top of the left column. "What word do you think I should write here?" I asked, pointing to the top of the right column, wanting to be explicit about setting up the chart. Oftentimes students are presented with abstract representations of information but don't have the chance to see how and why the information is organized in a particular way. Faced with blank stares, I continued, "What are we counting today?"

"Chicken legs!" several students said, giggling again.

"OK, then I think I should write 'Legs' here," I said, writing the word at the top of the right column.

Chickens	Legs

"Back when there was only one chicken, how many legs were there?" I asked, covering up two of the chickens I'd drawn.

"Two!" the class answered in unison.

"So if we have one chicken," I said, writing a *1* under Chickens, "there will be two legs." I wrote a *2* under Legs.

"What about when there were two chickens? How many legs were there then?" I asked, moving my hand so that two of the chickens on the board were visible. The students answered four legs, and again I wrote the numbers on the chart as I reiterated what they stood for.

"Now we're thinking about how many legs there are when we have three chickens," I said, writing the number *3* in the left-hand column and a question mark in the right-hand column.

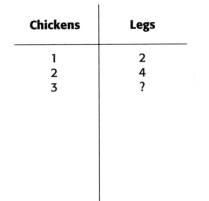

Chickens	Legs
1	2
2	4
3	?

"It's six. Three plus three is six," Damanjit said confidently. Intrigued, I wrote Damanjit's number sentence on the board. Although I wasn't sure how her equation fit in the context of the chicken legs, I was glad that she'd seen the doubling relationship between the chickens and the legs.

"How else can we be sure that there are six legs when we have three chickens?" I asked, wanting the students to share more of their thinking.

"I counted," Jose said.

"How did you count?" I asked.

"Like two, four, six," he said, holding up two fingers and pointing them toward the board. I wrote Jose's number sequence—*2, 4, 6*—under Damanjit's equation. Pointing to the chart, I erased the question mark and said, "Here's where I want to write the number of legs for three chickens. Give me a thumbs up if you think I should write a six." Thumbs went up and I recorded a 6.

Chickens	Legs
1	2
2	4
3	6

Pointing to the numbers in the right column, I commented, "Two, four, six. Those are the same numbers Jose said. I wonder why that is?"

Not really expecting an answer, I asked, "Is there another number sentence we could write to go with this picture?" I pointed to the three chickens.

"Two plus two plus two?" Raven asked.

"That makes sense to me," I commented as I wrote *2 + 2 + 2* on the board.

"And what does this equal?" I asked the class as I wrote an equals sign.

"Six!" several students answered loudly. I recorded a 6.

"Let's check with our fingers this time," I suggested. "Two fingers plus two more fingers is one, two, three, four fingers," I said, modeling with my own fingers. "Plus two more fingers is one, two, three, four, five, six!" I concluded. "Now I'm going to draw one more chicken on the board and I want you to raise your hand when you're ready to tell me how many legs there will be." I wrote a *4* in the left column of the chart and a question mark next to it in the right column. Several students shared their reasoning and I erased the question mark and wrote an *8*.

Chickens	Legs
1	2
2	4
3	6
4	8

"What do you notice about the numbers in our chart?" I asked.

"It's counting," Ralonte said, pointing to the Chickens column. "One, two, three, four."

"What do you think will come next after four?" I asked, seizing the opportunity to show that a pattern can be used to predict beyond the information you have at hand.

"Five," Ralonte answered.

"And then what?" I asked, addressing the whole class. "What if I wanted to keep going and going?"

"Six, seven, eight, nine, ten . . . !" answered the class in a crescendo of voices.

I gave my cue for quiet and said, "What else do you notice about the numbers in our chart?"

"Two, four, six, eight," Jose said, "like I was counting."

"It goes up by two," Alex commented.

"What if we wanted to keep going after eight?" I asked. "Let's count by twos . . . two, four, six, eight . . . " I stopped counting and several students kept going with varying accuracy.

"Today when you go back to your seats, I'd like you to keep going with our Chicken Leg Pattern. You can use pattern blocks, pictures, words, and numbers." I left some space on the chart and wrote a *10* under the Chickens column and a question mark next to it in the Legs column.

"I'd like you to figure out how many legs you think there would be if we had ten chickens," I said, pointing to the chart. "If you want to make your own chart like this, you can too."

Observing the Students   As I handed out paper, I gave students the choice of working alone or with a partner of their choice. As I watched students work, I was fascinated to see the variety of ways that they began. While Daria immediately made a pattern block chicken and began tracing it on her paper,

Khalia wrote the numbers from *1* to *10* and then began drawing chickens. She wrote: *How mine legs on the chickens.* After drawing the chickens, she counted the number of legs and recorded the information in sentences: *1 chicken is 2 legs, 2 chickens is 4 legs*, and so on. (See Figure 9–5.)

After making a version of a chicken with pattern blocks, Alex began recording the numbers of chickens and legs. After three and six, he ran into his drawing of the chicken and started his chart over on the other side of his paper. This time he wrote the numbers vertically and put a line between the columns. Alex skipped from four chickens to ten chickens and correctly listed the number of legs as twenty. When I asked him how he knew that there would be twenty legs for ten chickens he said, "Ten plus ten is twenty." I asked him how many legs he thought one hundred chickens would have and he answered, "Two hundred." I then asked him if he thought he could figure out the number of legs for any number of chickens and left him to think. (See Figure 9–6).

When I passed by Daria again, I saw that she had finished tracing her first pattern block chicken and written a *2* in its body. She had also finished tracing a second chicken and had written *2 + 2 = 4* at the bottom of her paper. By the time the period was over she had traced a third chicken, written a *6* in the body, and added the number sentence *2 + 2 + 2 = 6*. (See Figure 9–7.)

Priya and Sukhraj worked together meticulously, writing a sentence for each number of chickens and legs. At first I thought that they were figuring out the number of legs by counting in their heads or doubling the number of chickens. However, after watching them more closely, I saw that each time they were ready to write the number of legs they needed, they looked over at the carefully built row of pattern block chickens that Raven was building next to them. This observation reminded me how easy it is to make assumptions about how students figure things out. Once again I was reminded of the importance of careful observation and listening to students share their reasoning.

Khalia drew the chickens, counted the number of legs, and recorded the information.

Alex built a chicken with pattern blocks and then traced it. He recorded numbers above the chicken and then recorded them again on a T-chart. He listed the number of blocks for one, two, three, and four chickens, then skipped a space and recorded for ten chickens.

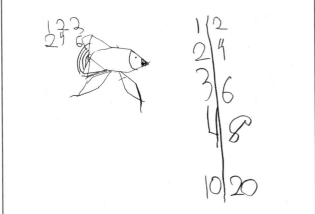

FIGURE 9–7 Daria figured out the number of legs for one, two, and three chickens, recording number sentences for two and three chickens.

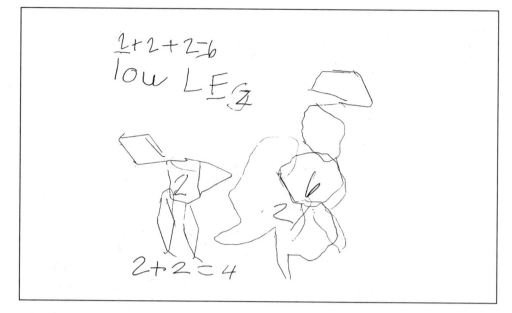

By the end of the period, Priya and Sukhraj had accurately listed the number of legs for one through six chickens. They had written *7 chicken legs is* when I interrupted the class to give directions for cleaning up. Later I noticed that they had completed the sentence: *7 chicken legs is 20 legs*. I wondered where they got that answer. My hunch was that they had heard others discussing that there were twenty legs for ten chickens and that they wanted to record the "right" answer, but I couldn't be sure and didn't have time to talk with them. (See Figure 9–8.)

FIGURE 9–8 Priya and Sukhraj worked together meticulously, writing a sentence for each number of chickens and legs. They wrote their last answer in haste at the end of the period, seemingly combining the problems of the number of legs for seven chickens and ten chickens.

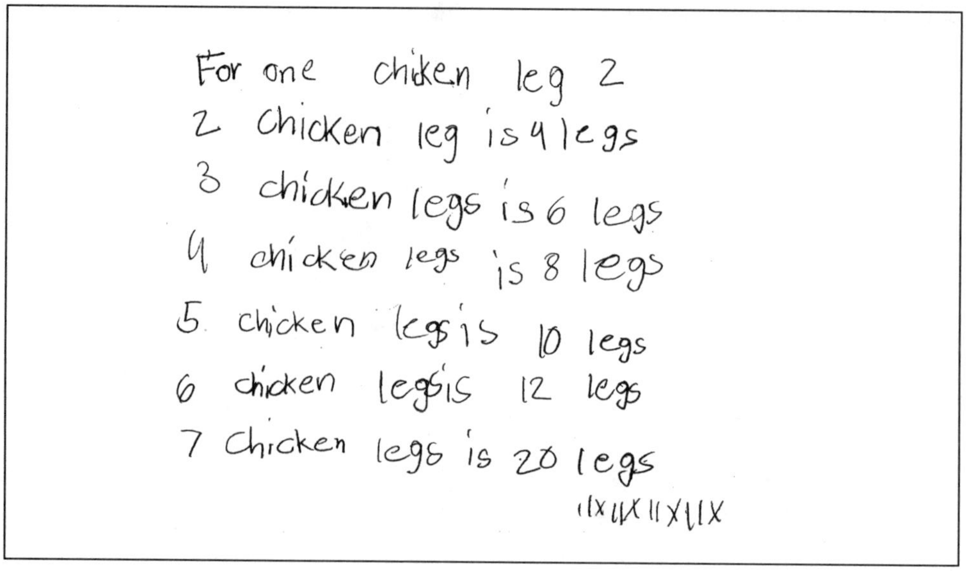

For one chiken leg 2
2 Chicken leg is 4 legs
3 chicken legs is 6 legs
4 chicken legs is 8 legs
5 chicken legs is 10 legs
6 chicken legs is 12 legs
7 Chicken legs is 20 legs

After the class had cleaned up and gone out for a welcome recess without rain, I looked through the rest of the papers. Jose was passionate about writing words and had, as usual, used all words to describe what he'd found: *We have to chickens and that make for.* Further down his paper, he'd written *3* and next to it, *six legs.* Figure 9–9 shows how one student recorded without drawing.

FIGURE 9-9 Precious recorded the pattern of chickens and legs on a T-chart. Even though her columns weren't lined up, she understood how the numbers paired.

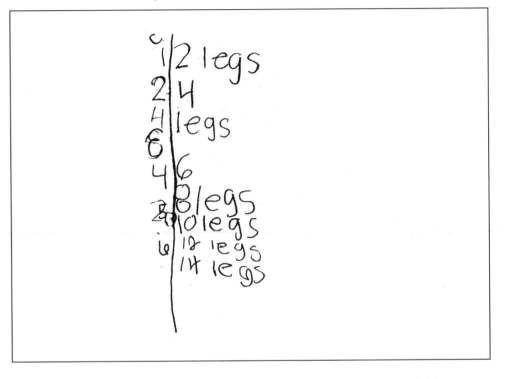

Extensions

Over the next several days, repeat the experience for chickens' eyes, beaks, and wings. Record T-charts on construction paper, post them on the wall, and ask children to compare them. Have them discuss why some charts are the same (the T-charts for beaks and tails, for example) and some are different (the T-charts for beaks and legs, for example).

On subsequent days, investigate cows, counting their tails, eyes, ears, and feet. Record on T-charts and talk about the patterns for each investigation.

CHAPTER 10

People Patterns

OVERVIEW

In this lesson, children explore number patterns that relate to their noses, eyes, fingers, and toes. For each pattern, the children record in two ways: on a T-chart and by shading in numbers on a 0–99 chart. They then write about the patterns they notice. The lesson helps build children's number sense as they investigate patterns in twos, fives, and tens.

BACKGROUND

The children need no previous experience for this lesson. If you haven't yet introduced them to recording on T-charts, however, you may need to explain how to do so more than was done with this particular class. However, children catch on easily to using T-charts from watching you demonstrate, so this will not take very long.

The lesson as described was taught on four consecutive days. On each day, the children figure out how many people are in class altogether, counting the teacher. On the first day, they explore the pattern of noses, figuring out how many noses there would be if no one were in the room, if one person were in the room, two people, three, four, and so on up to the number of people actually in the room. Then they extend the pattern for any number of people. On a 0–99 chart, the children shade in all the possible numbers of noses for any number of people, which means they shade in all of the numbers on the chart. Also, they record on a T-chart with the columns labeled *People* and *Noses*, writing the same numbers in both. The pattern of noses is obvious to the children and it's for that reason that it's a good introduction to this lesson. It builds children's confidence and helps them become familiar with the procedures for shading numbers on a 0–99 chart and recording on a T-chart.

On other days, the children repeat the experience for the number of eyes, fingers on one hand, and toes. This gives them experience with patterns of twos, fives, and tens. Finally, children compare the patterns and see what is the same and different about them.

The different parts of this lesson don't have to be taught on consecutive days, but it's a good idea to teach them in fairly close proximity so that children remember the procedures for investigating and recording. Also, you don't have to use all of the patterns; choose what you think is appropriate for your class. And you may prefer to have children record only on T-charts or only shade numbers on a 0–99 chart; again, decide what's appropriate for your class. The lesson as described was taught to second graders. For kindergarten children and some first graders, recording is inappropriate and it's sufficient either for you to record for the class or to point to the numbers on a large 0–99 chart as the pattern emerges.

VOCABULARY

pattern, T-chart

MATERIALS

- 0–99 charts, 4 per student and 4 for your demonstration

TIME

- four class periods

Day 1

The Lesson

"How many people are in this room?" I asked to begin the lesson. "I'm going to give you some time to think about it. Raise your hand when you know." Several hands went up immediately, but most children began counting each person in the room.

I waited until most of the students had raised a hand and said, "On the count of three, whisper your answer." I counted to three and in the loud whisper of voices, I detected several different answers. Asking children to respond together encourages participation without putting anyone on the spot.

"Now I'd like to hear how you figured out your answer," I said, without confirming or challenging any of the answers I'd heard. I've noticed that after students share their answers in unison, it seems easier for them to talk about how they thought about a problem. Also, a class response gives me an initial rough idea of what most students are thinking.

"I counted," Nadia said.

"Show us how you counted," I said.

Nadia counted the students in the room one by one, beginning with her partner, Eugene. When she finished she said, in a satisfied voice, "Nineteen!"

"What about you?" I asked, having watched carefully as she counted.

"Oh yeah! Twenty!" she responded. Although it took a minute or two to allow Nadia to show how she counted, it gave students who still weren't sure a chance to watch Nadia's careful counting and get a sense of the answer themselves.

"Who else figured out the number of people in the room the way Nadia did?" I asked. Several hands went up around the room.

"Did anyone figure it out a different way?" I asked.

"It's twenty because Richard's absent but we have to count you," Marlon said.

"Is anyone else absent?" I asked, looking around the room, hoping to draw the rest of the class into Marlon's thinking.

"No!" came a chorus of voices.

"Today it's nineteen kids," Navjot said enthusiastically.

"So why did Marlon say there are twenty people?" I asked.

"Because of you! We have to count *all* the people," Reginald said in a booming voice.

"I see," I said and moved on to ask, "How else could we figure out how many people are in the room?"

"We could count by twos," Marie suggested. Together we counted the students by twos and confirmed that there were exactly twenty people in the room. On the board I wrote:

There are 20 people in the room.

"Now I have a different question for you," I said, pausing for a moment to be sure they were all listening. "How many noses are there in the room? Raise your hand when you have an idea." Although many hands went up immediately, to give all of the students a chance to think, I took a moment to write on the board:

There are ? noses in the room.

After another few seconds I asked the students to whisper the answer on the count of three. "Twenty!" came the loud stage whisper.

"How did you know so fast?" I asked.

"Because we counted all the people and there are the exact same number of noses," Jared said.

I suggested, "Let's count noses just to make sure there are twenty." Together we counted and confirmed that there were indeed twenty noses in the room. I replaced the question mark in the sentence with 20:

There are 20 noses in the room.

Pointing to the two sentences I had written, I said in a thoughtful tone, "So when we counted people we got twenty, and when we counted noses we got twenty. I wonder why we got the same number both times?" In a way the answer to this question is obvious, but in another way it's complex. The students understand intuitively that the numbers are the same, but they don't necessarily have the ability to explain why. It's difficult for some to explain the generalization that the number of people is equal to the number of noses.

After several seconds of silence Marie said, "We only have one, so it's the same."

"I agree," I responded, and added with a smile, "Raise your hand if you have just one nose." There was a round of giggling and everyone raised a hand.

"Let's make a T-chart about people and noses," I said, drawing a large T-chart on the board and labeling the columns *People* and *Noses*.

People	Noses

"If no one was in the room, how many people would that be?" I asked.

"Not even you?" Carmen asked.

"No, what if it was evening and everyone was home eating dinner, even me. How many people would there be in the room?"

"Zero," Paulo said. I wrote a *0* in the left column.

"And how many noses would there be in the room if there weren't any people?" I asked.

"None if there's no people," Peter said matter-of-factly. I wrote a second *0* on the T-chart, in the right column.

"What if there was one person in the room? Suppose it was early in the morning when only I'm here before school starts," I said, writing a *1* in the People column. "How many noses then?"

"One," answered several voices. I wrote a *1* in the Noses column.

"And what about if two people were in the room?" I said, writing a *2* in the People column. "How many noses?"

"Two," came another enthusiastic answer. I continued this way until we'd recorded the number of noses for six people.

People	Noses
0	0
1	1
2	2
3	3
4	4
5	5
6	6

"Now I'm going to draw three dots going down in the People column. That means we're going to skip some numbers," I said, drawing three dots at the end of each column to indicate the omission. Also, I extended the vertical line of the T-chart to accommodate this new addition.

"How many noses for ten people?" I said, writing a *10* in the People column.

"Ten," Myles said.

"Give me a thumbs up if you agree with Myles," I said. Many thumbs went up.

"How did you know ten?" I asked.

"Because you said ten people," he responded.

"So you think it's going to be the same number?" I asked as I recorded *10* in the Noses column. Myles nodded. I drew three more dots and wrote *20* in the People column.

People	Noses
0	0
1	1
2	2
3	3
4	4
5	5
6	6
.	.
.	.
.	.
10	10
.	.
.	.
.	.
20	

"How many noses now?" I asked.

Latasha answered, "Twenty. We counted before." She pointed to the sentences I'd written on the board earlier. I wrote *20* on the Noses side of the T-chart.

"What do you notice about our T-chart for people and noses?" I asked.

"It's the same," Shivani said.

"What's the same?" I asked, pushing her to be more precise.

"The numbers are the same," she said, pointing to the T-chart.

"Zero people, zero noses, one person, one nose, two people, two noses, like that?" I said, pointing at the corresponding numbers on the T-chart. Shivani nodded.

"What else do you notice?" I asked, pressing the class for more observations.

"It's counting one, two, three, four, five, six," Bethany answered.

"Then what happened?" I said, pointing to the dots. "What do these dots mean?"

"We're skipping!" Lisa said.

"What if we wanted to keep going on our T-chart? How many noses would there be for twenty-one people?" I asked, writing *21* in the People column.

"Twenty-one," several students answered.

"And what about for twenty-two people?" I said, adding *22* to the chart.

"Twenty-two!" the class answered. Together we filled in the T-chart to 26. I paused and looked at the chart.

People	Noses
0	0
1	1
2	2
3	3
4	4
5	5
6	6
.	.
.	.
.	.
10	10
.	.
.	.
.	.
20	20
21	21
22	22
23	23
24	24
25	25
26	26

"But there aren't twenty-six people in this room. Are you sure it would be twenty-six noses?" I asked, pointing out that they'd gone beyond the information they could physically verify.

"Yes," the children chorused.

"We could keep going and going on the T-chart," I said, drawing three more dots. "What about fifty people?" I wrote *50* in the People column.

"It's fifty noses," Marie said. "It's just the same number every time."

"OK, so for one hundred people there would be . . . ?"

"One hundred noses!" the class answered.

"Everyone turn to your partner," I instructed. "One of you says a number of people, then your partner tells you how many noses there would be. Then you switch. When it's your turn, you can say any number of people you want." The class erupted into enthusiastic noise. I walked around the room, briefly listening to each pair of students. Paulo and Myles were taking turns saying the number of people. Paulo started with two hundred people. Myles answered two hundred noses and asked about five hundred people in return. Travis and Amy had a different approach. Travis said a number and Amy answered as fast as she could, giggling with each response.

After a moment I called the class back together and held up a 0–99 chart. "I want to shade in all the numbers of noses that could possibly be in the room on this zero to ninety-nine chart. Could there be zero noses in the room?" I asked. There was a quiet murmur of "yes."

"So I'm going to shade in 0 with the side of my pencil." I taped the chart on the chalkboard and shaded in zero. "What about one nose? Is that possible? Two noses? Three noses?" Each suggestion elicited a soft agreement.

"Now what if I keep going, shading in all the numbers I can for numbers of noses? What will my zero to ninety-nine chart look like when I'm done?" Faced with blank looks, I rephrased my question. "Do you think all of the numbers will be shaded in, or only some of the numbers? What will the chart look like if I keep going to the bottom?"

"It's going to be all shaded," Cameron said confidently.

"So we could have any number of noses from zero to ninety-nine?" I asked the class. Many heads nodded in agreement. I continued shading row by row, checking intermittent numbers aloud as I did so. "What about twenty noses? Could there be twenty noses? What about thirty-two noses? Could there be thirty-two noses?" I continued shading in the chart and eventually reached the last row and shaded in 99.

"What do you notice about the number of noses pattern?" I asked.

"It's all of the numbers," Nadia said.

"It's not a pattern, it's just everything," Marlon said, obviously concerned by my choice of words.

"Hmm, I agree that all the numbers are shaded in. If you look at the numbers that we shaded, could you tell what comes next after ninety-nine?" I asked.

"One hundred," whispered several students.

"I agree. That's how I know something is a pattern. If I can figure out what comes next, then I'm pretty sure there's a pattern," I said.

Sensing we'd done enough, I wrote *Noses* at the top of the 0–99 chart, drew a T-chart to the left to model for the children how they would be recording the next day, and ended the lesson.

Noses

People	Noses
0	0
1	1
2	2
3	3
.	.
.	.
.	.
99	99

0	1	2	3	4	5	6	7	8	9
10	11	12	13	14	15	16	17	18	19
20	21	22	23	24	25	26	27	28	29
30	31	32	33	34	35	36	37	38	39
40	41	42	43	44	45	46	47	48	49
50	51	52	53	54	55	56	57	58	59
60	61	62	63	64	65	66	67	68	69
70	71	72	73	74	75	76	77	78	79
80	81	82	83	84	85	86	87	88	89
90	91	92	93	94	95	96	97	98	99

Day 2

The next day I began the lesson by asking, "Can you figure out without counting how many people are in the room today?" Several children looked at me blankly while others began to count covertly.

"What about Marlon's idea from yesterday? He said there were twenty people in the room yesterday because one person was absent but you have to count me. Is anyone absent today?" I asked.

"Nobody is absent," Navjot said, carefully annunciating each word.

"It's twenty-one because nobody's sick," Latasha said.

"That sounds reasonable," I replied. "Let's count to make sure." Together we counted the number of people in the room and confirmed that there were twenty-one. On the board I wrote:

There are 21 people in the room.

"Yesterday we talked about people and noses," I said, pointing to the 0–99 chart from the day before. "Today I have a new question and I'm going to give you time to think about it by yourself. Raise your hand when you think you know. The question is, How many eyes are there in the room today?" Most of the students began quietly counting by twos, looking around the room and pointing to a new person as they said each new number in the sequence.

I noticed Navjot counting the number of eyes at her table and as I moved closer, I could hear her counting by ones. Several students at the table were sitting quietly. When I asked Bethany what she was thinking about, she whispered, "I don't get it!" I suggested counting and she replied, upset, "But I can't see everyone!" As I looked around the room from Bethany's vantage point, I noticed that although she could see each student, some were facing away from her.

"How many eyes do I have?" I whispered.

"Two," she answered, smiling.

"How many eyes do you have?" I continued in a low voice.

"Two," she replied.

"Do you think everybody has two eyes?" I asked.

Bethany thought for a moment and said "yes" in a tentative tone.

"So, maybe you can think about each person having two eyes and count their eyes even if you can't see their faces," I suggested, unsure if she would accept my advice.

"OK," she said, beginning to count the eyes of the people near her by ones. I wanted to wait and see what she would do when she got to the students who were turned away from her, but most of the students had their hands up and were beginning to get restless. So that I could continue watching Bethany, I directed the students to share their answers with someone near them. However, the sudden noise distracted Bethany and she stopped counting.

I then called the class to attention and asked for a volunteer to suggest how we could figure out the answer. Lisa suggested first, "Count by twos." Together we counted around the room by twos and got the answer of forty-two eyes.

Paulo then suggested, "Count two numbers on each person." I asked him to demonstrate and he pointed to the person across from him, saying, "One, two." He then pointed to the next person at his table, saying, "Three, four."

By the time he got to ten the class had joined in and we again counted together to forty-two eyes. I wrote on the board:

There are 42 eyes in the room.

"I'm going to give each of you a zero to ninety-nine chart and we'll all shade in the number of eyes that are possible and see if we notice a pattern. Don't start yet. Wait until everyone has a chart and then we'll start together." I posted a blank 0–99 chart on the chalkboard and distributed one to each child.

"If there were zero people in the room, how many eyes would there be?" I began.

"Zero!" many voices answered. I shaded in 0 with the side of my pencil and directed the children to do the same. I checked to be sure that they all followed my direction.

"If there were one person in the room, how many eyes would there be?" I asked.

"Two," the class answered. I shaded in 2 and waited for the children to do the same.

"If there were two people in the room, how many eyes would there be?"

"Four," they answered. I shaded in 4 and paused for them to do so.

Before continuing with the pattern, I asked, "Why couldn't we shade in the number one?" After a brief pause I continued. "Could someone have just one eye?"

"Yes, if something happened," Jared suggested.

"Like a pirate!" Peter said.

"You're right. Someone could have an accident and lose an eye, but for today let's just think about people that have two eyes," I suggested. Peter covered up one eye with his hand and made pirate noises.

"No pirates today," I said and he put his hand down.

"What about three?" I asked, pointing to the unshaded number. "Why didn't we shade three?"

"'Cause it's going by twos?" Amy said tentatively.

"And do you land on three when you're counting by twos?" I asked, agreeing with her. Amy shook her head. I suggested that we keep going and see how the counting by twos pattern would continue.

I motioned for three students to come to the front of the room and asked, "How many eyes for three people?" Together we counted by twos to six. I shaded in 6 on the 0–99 chart and waited for the children to shade in 6 on their charts. I motioned for one more person to come forward. Together we counted to eight, and then we shaded in 8 on our 0–99 charts. I asked the four students at the front of the room to return to their seats and I gave them a moment to shade the 6 and 8 on their charts.

"Now it's your turn. Keep going and fill in your zero to ninety-nine chart as far as you can for numbers of eyes," I said, writing the word *Eyes* at the top of the 0–99 chart. "I'd also like you to make a T-chart on the side of your chart that shows people and eyes," I said, drawing a T-chart to the left of the 0–99 chart and labeling the columns *People* and *Eyes*.

People	Eyes
0	0
1	2
2	4
3	6

Eyes

0	1	2	3	4	5	6	7	8	9
10	11	12	13	14	15	16	17	18	19
20	21	22	23	24	25	26	27	28	29
30	31	32	33	34	35	36	37	38	39
40	41	42	43	44	45	46	47	48	49
50	51	52	53	54	55	56	57	58	59
60	61	62	63	64	65	66	67	68	69
70	71	72	73	74	75	76	77	78	79
80	81	82	83	84	85	86	87	88	89
90	91	92	93	94	95	96	97	98	99

On the board I drew a larger version of the T-chart, labeling the columns *People* and *Eyes*. I wrote a *0* in the People column and asked, "How many eyes do zero people have?"

"Zero," they answered, and I wrote a *0* in the Eyes column.

I then wrote a *1* in the People column and asked, "How many eyes does one person have?"

"Two," they answered, and I wrote a *2* in the Eyes column.

I repeated this for two and three people. I felt comfortable that the children knew how to record on the T-chart, so I gave one last direction: "When you're done, write about what you notice."

Observing the Students Students began working and I circulated, watching how they approached the investigation. Marie immediately began shading every other column of numbers. As I walked past, she looked up at me with a worried look on her face. "Is zero an even number?" she asked, pointing to her paper.

"It looks like zero fits your pattern. What do you think?" Marie shrugged her shoulders and looked to me for an answer.

"Are the other numbers you shaded even?" I asked. Marie nodded.

"How do you know if a number is even if you don't have the chart?" I asked.

"You count by twos," she answered.

"I agree," I said, "and when we count by twos on the chart, we skip every other number." I demonstrated for Marie, pointing to each space on the first row of her 0–99 chart as I skip-counted: "Two, skip, four, skip, six, skip, eight, skip."

"We can count backward, too," I continued. "Count with me." I put Marie's finger on the 8 and skip-counted backward with her: "Eight, skip, six, skip, four, skip, two, skip, zero. Zero fits the pattern. That's one way I know it's an even number." Marie went back to shading in her 0–99 chart, apparently satisfied with my answer, but I knew that she needed many more experiences to understand all of zero's particular characteristics.

In a while I checked back with Marie and she'd filled out her T-chart to eight people and sixteen eyes, apparently feeling that that was enough to show

CHAPTER 12

Pattern Block Trees

OVERVIEW

In this lesson, students investigate the growth pattern of trees built from pattern blocks. Three blocks—a square, a trapezoid, and a triangle—are used to build a one-year-old tree. A two-year-old tree uses five blocks— two squares, two trapezoids, and a triangle. Then, as the tree grows each year, it adds another square and another trapezoid but always has one triangle on top. The children investigate the pattern by building the trees, recording the number of blocks on a T-chart, describing how the pattern is growing, and then predicting the number of blocks needed for a hundred-year-old tree.

BACKGROUND

Children need no previous experience for this lesson. It's suitable as an introductory activity with a growth pattern or as an activity for students who have had previous experiences with growth patterns. The lesson also introduces or reinforces for children how to record information about a pattern on a T-chart.

In this pattern, part of the tree stays the same as it grows—the triangle on top. Part of the pattern changes—the number of squares and trapezoids. While we don't make it explicit for the children, the lesson gives them experience with identifying both the variable and constant parts of a growth pattern.

The lesson as described was taught to second graders. Adjust the lesson so it's appropriate for your students. For example, second graders can build the pattern, record on a T-chart, describe the pattern, and think about how to extend the pattern to a tree that is one hundred years old. Ask first graders to build and record the pattern and perhaps also to describe how the pattern is growing. With kindergarten children, concentrate on having them just build the trees, or count the number of blocks in trees as you build them and describe how to build the next tree each time. Also, it isn't essential to extend the pattern to a hundred-year-old tree for either first graders or kindergarten children.

This lesson gives children experience thinking about odd numbers and also gives them practice with addition.

VOCABULARY

pattern, square, T-chart, trapezoid, triangle

MATERIALS

- pattern blocks, 1 bucket for each table

TIME

- one to two class periods

The Lesson

I asked for the children's attention and began, "Today we're going to use the pattern blocks to make something that grows." I held up a square, a trapezoid, and a triangle arranged to look like a tree.

"What does this look like to you?" I asked, making sure everyone could see.

"A rocket!" Peter said.

"An arrow," Latasha said.

"A tree," Carmen said.

"I agree it looks like lots of things, but I was thinking of a tree when I built it. For today let's use our imaginations and call this a tree. Since it's hard to see my blocks from far away, I'm going to draw my tree on the board," I said, repeating the names of the shapes as I drew them.

"Now this tree isn't very tall, is it? This tree is actually a very young tree. It's only one year old," I said. I wrote *1 year old* to the left of the tree.

"After a year goes by and the tree gets rained on and the sun shines on it, here's what it looks like when it's two years old," I said, drawing and labeling a two-year-old tree.

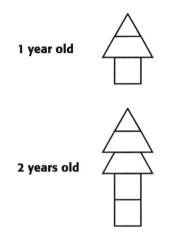

1 year old

2 years old

"What do you notice?" I asked.

"It's bigger," Bethany said.

"It growed," Beatriz said.

"If you were going to build your own one-year-old tree, what blocks would you need from the tub?" I asked, pointing to the first tree.

"A square and a triangle and a hexagon," Reginald said confidently.

"I see the square," I said, pointing, "and I see the triangle, but what's this red shape called?" I touched the trapezoid and looked across the room at the shapes poster on the wall.

Several voices called out, "Trapezoid."

"What if you wanted to make your own two-year-old tree just like mine? What blocks would you need?" I asked, pointing to the second tree.

"Two trapezoids," Reginald shouted out quickly.

"And two squares," Latasha added.

"What about the triangle? Do you need two of those, too?" I asked.

"No, it just has one," Travis said.

"Look at the one-year-old tree and the two-year-old tree and think about what you think a three-year-old tree is going to look like," I said. "You can close your eyes and imagine the blocks in your head if you want to." I covered my eyes with the palms of my hands for a moment to demonstrate. After a moment for quiet thinking, I said, "Now I'm going to show you what a three-year-old tree looks like. When I'm done, raise your hand if it looks like what you imagined." I wrote *3 years old* on the board and drew a three-year-old tree with three squares, three trapezoids and one triangle. Most of the children raised a hand when I finished. I suspected that some of them hadn't predicted exactly what I drew, but this wasn't as important as giving students a chance to predict and visualize.

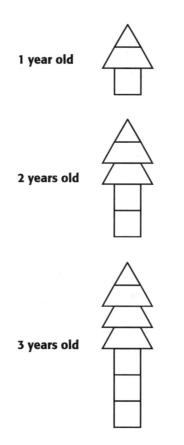

1 year old

2 years old

3 years old

"How is the tree growing?" I asked.

"It's getting taller and taller. It's growing up," Amy said.

"It's got *three* squares and *three* trapezoids and one triangle," Lisa said, with emphasis on the threes.

"It adds one trapezoid and one square each time," Cameron commented.

"In a moment you'll return to your seats and I'll set out pattern blocks at each table. What you're to do is build a four-year-old tree," I said. As the children returned to their seats, I distributed the pattern blocks.

Students quickly began pulling blocks out of the tubs. Some students built just the four-year-old tree as I had asked. Several others began by building a one-year-old tree, then built two-, three-, and four-year-old trees. Some scooped out large handfuls of blocks and then sorted out the squares, trapezoids, and triangles they needed. Others picked out each block as they needed it, constructing trees one block at a time. Some students began constructing trees from the bottom up, starting with the squares, adding the trapezoids, and finally placing the triangle. Others started with the triangle and worked their way down, and a few students began in the middle with the trapezoids.

When almost all of the students had built a four-year-old tree, I interrupted the class. I said, "Please stop working for a moment and listen to some directions. I know it's hard to listen with all of those blocks in front of you, but please put your hands in your lap and give me your attention." I waited a moment until I had all of the children's attention. These children complied with my request, but I've taught classes in which the students are too distracted by the blocks to listen. When this occurs, I ask the students to put the blocks away first.

"Today we're going to investigate how this pattern block tree grows. To help us we're going to write down the number of blocks the tree has each year," I said, drawing a T-chart on the board.

"When the tree was one year old, how many blocks did it have?" I asked, writing a *1* in the left column. "Let's count together from the bottom block up." The children counted with me as we counted first the square, then the trapezoid, and finally the triangle. I counted up from the bottom because I thought it would help the children see that the number of squares and trapezoids increased each year, but there was always one triangle at the top. The number of squares and trapezoids varied, but the one triangle remained the same. It's helpful when students are investigating growth patterns to think about what the variable part of the pattern is and if there is a part of the pattern that remains constant. I wrote a *3* in the right column of the T-chart.

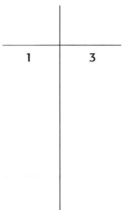

"What about the two-year-old tree?" I asked, writing a *2* in the left column. "How many blocks did it have?" We counted the blocks and I wrote a *5* in the right column. In the same way, we counted and recorded that the three-year-old tree had seven blocks.

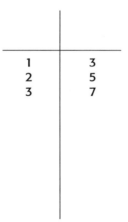

"What do you notice about the numbers in our T-chart?" I asked the class.

"They're counting, one, two, three," Navjot said.

"I see that, too," I said, pointing to the numbers in the left column. "I'm going to label that column *Years* so we can remember that those numbers tell us how old each tree is." I wrote *Years* at the top of the left column and then pointed to the right column. "This side was where we wrote how many blocks in each tree, so I'm going to write *Blocks* up here to help us remember what these numbers tell us." My goal was to connect the language, numbers, and T-chart recording very explicitly. For this reason, I didn't label the columns of the T-chart at first, but rather waited until I could involve the students in seeing how the labels connected to what they were building. I've found that this procedure helps keep the recording from getting too abstract.

Years	Blocks
1	3
2	5
3	7

"There's three there and three there," Richard said, pointing to the 3 at the end of the *Years* column and at the top of the *Blocks* column.

"It's skipping," Shivani said, pointing to the right column.

"Tell me what you mean," I said, wanting to know more about Shivani's idea.

"The three and then four but it's not four. It's skipping to the other number, it's five," Shivani explained. Shivani was just learning English. Her choice of words wasn't perfect but her idea was clear.

"Ah, so after three we skipped four and wrote five. And then we skipped six and wrote seven," I said to clarify Shivani's idea. She nodded her agreement.

"When I sent you to your seats I asked you to build a four-year-old tree," I said, writing *4* in the left column. "Everyone silently count the blocks in your four-year-old tree and raise your hand when you know how many blocks there are." After a few seconds I asked students to whisper the answer on the count of three.

"Nine," came the loud whisper. I wrote *9* in the right column and asked Shivani if it fit her pattern. She smiled and nodded in agreement. I drew a four-year-old tree on the board.

"How many blocks do you think will be in a five-year-old tree?" I asked, writing a *5* and a question mark across the next row of the T-chart.

Years	Blocks
1	3
2	5
3	7
4	9
5	?

After a brief pause, several hands went up.

"I think eleven," Marlon said.

"I agree. Why eleven?" I asked.

"Because you have to add one more square and one more trapezoid," he answered.

"I think the same thing," Amy commented, "because you add one more square and one more trapezoid and keep the triangle the same."

"Four plus one equals five and five plus five is ten and ten plus one is eleven," Cameron said in one breath. I paused for a moment, giving myself a chance to digest what Cameron had said.

"Can you tell us your idea again and tell what blocks you're talking about?" I asked, hoping this would help.

"For the squares, it's four plus one is five, and the same for the trapezoids," he began.

"Ah, four squares from before, plus one more in the new tree?" I asked, remembering his comment earlier in the lesson.

Cameron nodded. "It's the same for the trapezoids," he added.

I drew a column of four squares, counting as I went, paused, then drew one more square on top. "So there's four squares plus one more square," I commented, drawing a bracket next to the first four squares. I repeated the process for the trapezoids, bracketing the first four.

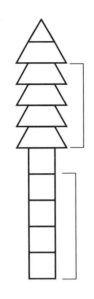

"Then you said five plus five is ten?" I asked. Cameron nodded. Scanning the room to see if the class was still with us, I continued.

"So we have five squares plus five trapezoids," I said, pausing to let Cameron continue.

"That's ten, and then one triangle makes eleven," he concluded.

"So for a five-year-old tree we could add five plus five plus one," I commented. I wrote on the board next to the drawing of the five-year-old tree:

5 + 5 + 1 = 11

"Could we add four plus four plus one for a four-year-old tree?" I asked, and wrote on the board:

4 + 4 + 1 = ?

After pausing a moment to let children consider my question, I continued, speaking slowly to let the students add with me. "Let's see, four plus four is eight, plus one is nine." I replaced the question mark with a *9*:

4 + 4 + 1 = 9

"Let's check the T-chart." I pointed to the numbers 4 and 9 on the T-chart and said, "Yep, the four-year-old tree has nine blocks!"

"Let's count the blocks on the four-year-old tree I drew on the board just to make sure," I continued. The children and I counted the blocks in the drawing of the four-year-old tree and verified that there were nine. We counted the blocks in the drawings for the three-year-old, two-year-old, and one-year-old trees, and I wrote the addition sentences on the board:

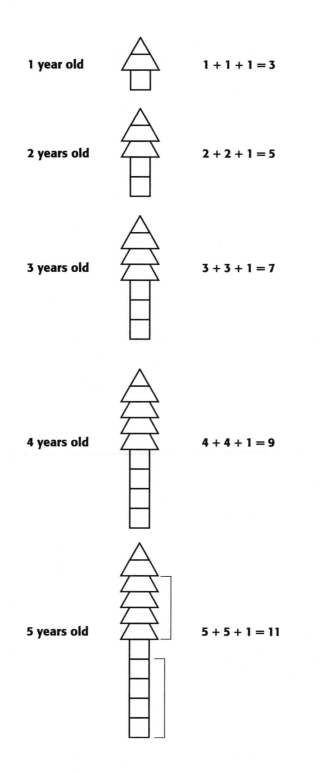

1 year old   1 + 1 + 1 = 3

2 years old   2 + 2 + 1 = 5

3 years old   3 + 3 + 1 = 7

4 years old   4 + 4 + 1 = 9

5 years old   5 + 5 + 1 = 11

"Let's try to figure out the number of blocks in a six-year-old tree," I said. I wrote on the board below the number sentence for the five-year-old tree:

6 + 6 + 1 = ?

Together we figured six plus six was twelve, plus one more was thirteen. I replaced the question mark with *13* and recorded *6* and *13* on the T-chart.

Years	Blocks
1	3
2	5
3	7
4	9
5	11
6	13

"Does thirteen fit the pattern of blocks?" I asked. "Three, five, seven, nine, eleven, thirteen. Shivani said the pattern skipped a number each time. Let's check. *Three*, skip four, *five*, skip six, *seven*, skip eight, *nine*, skip ten, *eleven*, skip twelve, *thirteen*! It fits!" The students cheered.

In some classes, what we had just done takes up most of a period and I wait for the next day to continue. But in this class, we had moved quickly and we had the option of extending the math period, so I continued.

A Class Assignment   I said to the class, "Now I'm going to hand out paper. Listen carefully to what you'll do. First, make a T-chart that shows how the tree grows, just as I did on the board. Next, write a sentence about how the tree grows. And then think about how many blocks would be in a tree that was one hundred years old." I stopped for a moment and then repeated, "A T-chart, a sentence, and then think about the number of blocks in a hundred-year-old tree." (I felt that most of the children in this class would be able to think about the problem of the hundred-year-old tree, but in some classes, I don't include this problem in the assignment.)

I didn't give the class any directions about using the blocks to build the trees. I assumed that some children would choose to do so, and that was fine with me, but building the trees wasn't essential. Also, drawing the trees wasn't essential, but it was fine if children wanted to do so. I think it's important to allow students to approach an assignment in ways that make sense to them.

Observing the Students   As I had predicted, several students constructed trees with the pattern blocks, while others began by recording on their papers. I circulated, clearing extra blocks from the students' tables.

I watched Reginald carefully divide his paper to make four boxes along the right side. He then began drawing a one-year-old tree in the first box. When I checked back later, he'd drawn two-, three-, and four-year-old trees, one in each of the boxes. He was working on his T-chart by that time, carefully checking each set of numbers by counting the blocks in the appropriate tree.

A problem soon occurred in the class. Some students were building taller and taller trees and there was an outcry that they needed more blocks. This created the opportunity for me to encourage students to look for ways to continue their work besides actually building the trees. I reminded them that earlier we'd figured out how many blocks were in the next tree by looking at the patterns in the numbers and by thinking about how the tree grew.

Reginald continued his T-chart to the bottom of his paper, made a new T-chart next to it, and continued recording. After recording that a fourteen-year-old tree had twenty-nine blocks, he drew several dots and stopped. On the back of his paper he wrote: *100 + 100 + 1 = 201*. He added this information to his T-chart and wrote: *The tree keeps on adding squares trapezoids and triangle stay the same.* (See Figure 12–1.)

On her T-chart, Beatriz drew a short horizontal line connecting each pair of numbers. After borrowing blocks from her tablemates she was able to make a nine-year-old tree. She counted to find it had seventeen blocks. She wrote: *I figet out with the blocks.*

Peter was sitting across from Reginald and divided his paper much the way Reginald did. He drew one- and two-year-old trees on his paper, then made a T-chart showing trees and blocks from one to seven years old. He wrote: *I made a tree and added more and more bloks.* Peter also wrote about how he was thinking about the tree growing: *I think that the tree has somthink in the tree is a sced that maks it grow or a egg or tree seeds.* His sentence reminded me that students often bring meaning to ideas in ways I hadn't expected.

Other students also wrote descriptions of how they saw the tree growing. Travis, for example, wrote: *The tree grows by adding more squares and more trapezoid and but you cant add more triangle.*

Marie wrote: *Like if you had a birthday you grow. So the tree grows when it is the tree's birthday.* (See Figure 12–2 on the following page.) To describe how she figured out the number of blocks in a hundred-year-old

FIGURE 12–1   Reginald started his T-chart in the middle of the paper. He ran out of room and continued with another T-chart to the left. On the back of the paper, he wrote about how he saw the tree growing.

tree, Marie then wrote: *If you made a 100 year old tree it is going to take 201 blocks. There will be 100 squares and there will be 100 trapezoids. When you add them you will have 201 blocks.* Marie didn't write about the triangle on top but accounted for it in her figuring.

Richard had a different way to express the same idea. He wrote: *100 year old tree has 201 blocks 100 □ 100 △ 1 △. Why? First I used 200 but I did not count the △ and it was 201.*

To figure out the number of blocks for a hundred-year-old tree, Peter correctly listed *100 square 100 trapezoids one triangle.* He added one hundred and one hundred to get two hundred, but when he added on the one triangle, he recorded his final answer as *2001,* writing the number as he said to himself, "Two hundred one." This is a common error for children whose understanding of place value is fragile.

Myles wrote: *100 + 100 = 200 because 1 + 1 = 2 and 0 + 0 = 0 and 50 + 50 = 100 and if you want oner* [another] *100 = 200 and with a triangle it will be 201.* (See Figure 12–3.)

I watched as Lisa struggled with this problem. First she wrote:

```
 100
+100
  +1
-----
```

FIGURE 12–2

Marie correctly figured out that there would be 201 blocks for a 100-year-old tree. She counted the one triangle even though she omitted it from her explanation.

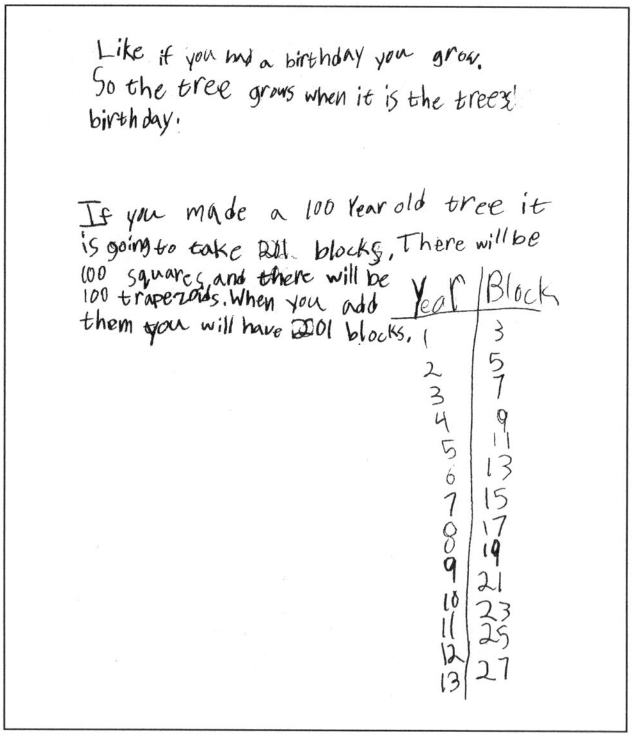

FIGURE 12–3

Myles drew several of the trees and recorded the number of blocks for trees from one to six years old. He also wrote about how he knew that a 100-year-old tree would have 201 blocks.

After looking for a long time at what she had written, she wrote: *I can not do 100.* Lisa stopped and looked some more. Then she began to draw a sketch of a tree. In the part that represented the squares she wrote *100*, in the trapezoid part she wrote *100*, and in the triangle she wrote *1*. She thought for a moment and wrote a number sentence: *200 + 1 = 201.*

I had a feeling that Lisa's first attempt had come from trying to add numbers in a column. After she wrote the numbers, she was confused because the 1 was in the wrong column. I interrupted Lisa and pointed to the column of numbers she had written. "You can do it this way, but the one has to be over here," I said, pointing to where the 1 should be. Lisa stared at her paper for a few seconds and wrote *201* under the problem. At the top of her paper she erased what she had written (*I can not do 100*) and wrote: *I had it the frst time.*

As usual, Latasha and Cameron finished early. I asked them to think about how many blocks they would need for any tree if they knew how old it was. Both of them were able to generalize! Cameron wrote: *If there was any number to make a tree I would just put how many trapezoids and squares and one triangle.* Latasha wrote: *I would add the same number then add 1.* (See Figure 12–4.)

A few minutes before the end of the period I interrupted the class and gave directions for cleaning up. Many students had kept the pattern blocks out as they worked and now blocks were spread on the floor, under papers, and on chairs. I don't like to see the room in a mess, but I also didn't want to interrupt the children as they were thinking and working. As the students worked to return the room to order, I decided that the mess had been well worth it.

Figure 12–5 shows how one other student worked on this activity.

FIGURE 12–4 Latasha clearly explained how she figured out the number of blocks in a 100-year-old tree. On the back of her paper, she wrote a generalization about how she would figure out the number of blocks in any tree and illustrated her idea for a 101-year-old tree.

FIGURE 12–5   After constructing a few trees with pattern blocks, Shivani correctly recorded on a T-chart without drawing the trees on her paper. She wrote about the pattern of the number of blocks.

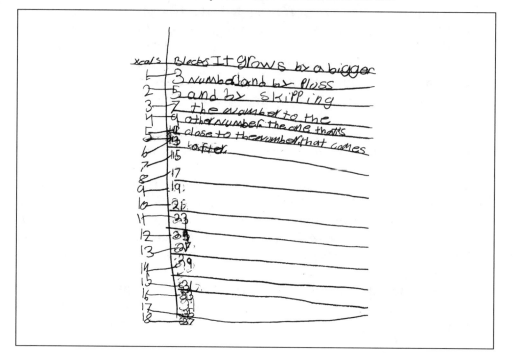

CHAPTER 13

Magic Machines

OVERVIEW

In this lesson, children are introduced to a "magic machine" that follows a rule to change items put into the machine into other items that come out of the machine. To begin, one circle is put into the machine and two circles come out, then a triangle is put in and two triangles come out, and so on for other shapes. The children guess what the machine is doing and also learn how to record the information on a T-chart. The children then investigate several examples of what happens when the controls on the machine are adjusted so it follows a different rule. They then create rules of their own. On the second day, the class examines patterns where numbers, not shapes, are put into the machine. They then create their own rules for numbers, record them, and describe them.

BACKGROUND

The magic machine introduces students to the idea of functions. By considering what the machine can do to shapes, and then to letters, students learn that setting the controls on the machine establishes a rule that acts in the same way on each item put into the machine. Also, for every item put in, there's only one possible output. The children also learn to record inputs and their resulting outputs on T-charts and describe the rules that the machine follows.

The students then think about rules for which numbers are the inputs and outputs. Examining various rules that the machine can follow for numbers gives the students experience with looking for numerical patterns, performing mental calculations, and making conjectures.

While this lesson introduces children to the idea of what a function is, it doesn't introduce or use the term *function*. Rather, it relies on the context of the magic machine and its controls. If you're not familiar with functions, however, read the background information in the Appendix for a more detailed explanation of the underlying mathematics.

This lesson is similar to the lesson based on the children's book *Two of Everything* (see Chapter 6), providing a similar experience through a different context. Although the lessons in these chapters are similar, both are engaging for children and the different contexts are useful for providing different approaches to the same mathematical idea. The lesson as described was taught to second graders and is also appropriate for first graders. For kindergarten children, you can introduce the magic machines to the children as described in the Day 1 section of the lesson.

VOCABULARY

pattern, T-chart

MATERIALS

- none

TIME

- two class periods

The Lesson | Day 1

I gathered the class on the carpet in front of the board and announced that we would be doing something new in math class today. On the board, I drew the following:

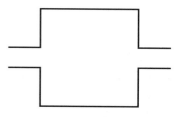

I said, "This is a special machine. I'm going to put a shape into the machine. Watch what comes out." I drew a small circle next to the opening on the left side of the machine and two circles next to the opening on the right side of the machine.

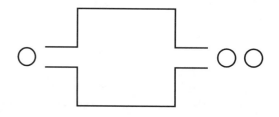

"Who can tell what the machine did?" I asked. No one volunteered. "What went into the machine?" I asked.

"A circle," Latasha said.

"Maybe it's a ball," Paulo said.

"Both of those are good ideas," I responded. "And what came out of the machine?"

Several children had ideas: "Two of them." "Two circles." "Two balls." "It made it double."

"Now I'm going to put a different shape into the machine," I said, erasing the circles and drawing a small triangle next to the opening on the left side of the machine. "The machine is going to do the same thing to the triangle that it did to the circle," I said, drawing two triangles next to the opening on the right side of the machine.

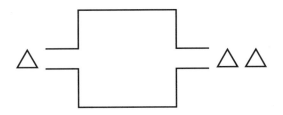

A few children made comments: "Now there are two triangles." "It doubled again."

"What other shape would you like me to put into the machine?" I asked.

"A diamond!" Myles suggested. It's common for children to use the term *diamond* when referring to a rhombus or even a square oriented with a corner up. I didn't correct Myles's word, but just erased the triangles and drew a rhombus on the left side of the machine.

"Hmm," I said, "when we put a circle into the machine, out came two circles. When we put a triangle in, out came . . . "

"Two triangles!" several children responded.

"I keep erasing what went in and what came out," I said. "I think we should write down what happened so far." I then gave the class two reasons for recording: "Writing down information helps us remember what happened. Also, writing can help us figure out what the machine is doing to the shapes we put in."

I drew a T-chart on the board. This particular class had recorded on T-charts before, but even if they hadn't, I've found that children catch on quickly to how to use them. I pointed to the left side of the chart and said, "In this column we can list all the shapes we put into the machine." I wrote *In* at the top of the column and pointed to the right side of the chart. "In this column we can write down what comes out of the machine," I said, writing *Out* at the top of the right column.

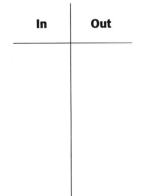

I then drew a circle in the left column of the T-chart and asked, "When we put a circle into the machine, what came out?"

"Two circles," the class responded.

I drew two circles in the right column, drew a triangle under the circle in the In column, and asked, "When we put a triangle in, what came out?"

"Two triangles," answered several students. I drew the two triangles.

"Now Myles told us to put a diamond into the machine," I said, drawing a rhombus under the triangle in the left column.

In	Out
◯	◯◯
△	△△
◇	

"Raise your hand if you know what's going to come out," I instructed, pointing to the right side of the machine. At this point I wanted to make sure that the class saw the connection between the machine and the information listed on the T-chart. Many hands went up and I asked the students to whisper their answer to someone near them. I heard many say "two diamonds." "On the count of three, let's whisper the answer . . . one, two, three," I instructed.

"Two diamonds!" came the stage whisper.

I drew two rhombuses coming out of the machine and asked, "Where should I record the two diamonds on our T-chart?"

"On the Out side," Bethany said, pointing to the chart.

"For the ones coming out," Marlon added. I drew the two rhombuses in the Out column and then asked for another shape to put in the machine. Nadia suggested a square. I erased the rhombuses and drew a square going into the machine. Again the students whispered the answer. I drew two squares coming out of the machine and recorded on the T-chart.

In	Out
◯	◯◯
△	△△
◇	◇◇
▢	▢▢

"Now let's look at what's happened so far," I said, pointing to the T-chart. "What do you think the machine is doing to the shapes we put in?" I waited until many hands were up before calling on Marie.

"It's cloning it," she said. I suddenly felt very old.

"It makes shapes turn into two shapes," Paulo said.

"It's making the same shape two times," Peter said.

"It's a copying machine," Latasha said.

I agreed that those were all good ways to describe what the machine was doing. "Now I'm going to adjust the machine so that it does something different to what goes in," I said. "Watch what happens now." I wrote a capital *A* going into the machine and a lowercase *a* coming out. I erased them both and wrote a capital *B* going in and a lowercase *b* coming out.

"Make a T-chart," Lisa suggested. I took her suggestion and recorded what had happened so far. If Lisa hadn't made the suggestion, I would have done so after another letter or two. I erased the shapes on the T-chart and entered the letters.

In	Out
A	a
B	b

"What if we put a capital *C* into the machine?" I asked, writing a *C* on the T-chart. The students answered and I continued with *D* and *E*, recording only on the T-chart and not showing the letters going into and coming out of the machine. Now that the class had the idea of the machine, I wanted to show them that they could just think about what was happening to the letters, without actually writing them next to the machine. The machine is an imaginary context that facilitates children's thinking about the relationship between two sets of objects. Once children are familiar with the context, they're able to understand the more abstract recording on a T-chart.

"What do you think the machine is doing this time?" I asked.

"It's a shrinker," Cameron said.

"It's making the big letters small," Jared said.

I told the class that I was going to adjust the machine again. I erased the letters near the machine and on the T-chart. This time I recorded on the T-chart first. "This time I'm going to put in a little circle," I said. "Out comes a big circle." I recorded the shapes as I spoke. "Next I'm going to put in a little square, and out comes a big square." I recorded these shapes on the T-chart.

In	Out
○	◯
□	☐

"What do you think happens next?" I called on Nadia, whose hand was waving wildly.

"A little tiny rectangle and a *big* rectangle," she said, making her voice high-pitched and then low to accentuate the size of the shapes as I had done. I recorded her suggestion. Then I recorded Lisa's suggestion to make a little heart and a big heart and Marlon's suggestion to make a teeny tiny triangle and a giant triangle.

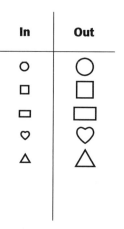

"What do you think the machine is doing this time?" I asked.

"It's the reverse," said Richard. Not sure what he meant I said, "Tell me more about that."

"The other one was getting smaller; this one is getting bigger," he responded. I realized that he was comparing the small and large shapes with the uppercase and lowercase letters we'd done before.

I gave one more example of a new setting for the machine, this time putting in outlines of shapes and having them come out shaded. I used pattern block shapes—a square, a triangle, a rhombus, a trapezoid, and a hexagon. Again I began by making the T-chart and didn't bother to draw the shapes going into and coming out of the machine.

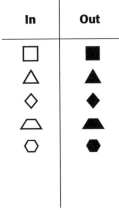

In	Out
□	■
△	▲
◇	◆
▱	◣
⬡	⬢

When I asked Cameron why it made sense for a shaded hexagon to come out of the machine as he'd suggested, he explained, "Because all the other ones were colored so the next shape should be colored." Cameron understood that once the machine is set, it does the same to whatever is put into it. That's the basis of understanding a function rule, but I didn't use the term *function* with the children.

A Class Assignment   Feeling confident that the students were ready to work on their own, I said, "Now you'll have a chance to make your own machines and your own T-charts to record what happened. Before I dismiss you to return to your seats, think about what you want your machine to do. When you have an idea, raise your hand." I waited until most of the students had a hand up and then asked them to whisper their idea to someone near them. I find it's helpful to give students a chance to begin thinking about what they're going to do before transitioning to independent work time. I also wanted to give students a chance to hear other ideas as well as to put their thoughts into words before they began writing. I excused the children to go to their tables and handed out paper.

Observing the Students   Latasha drew a machine at the top of her paper and a T-chart in the middle. She drew a small circle going into her machine and a large circle coming out. She recorded the circles on her T-chart and erased the circles from the sides of the machine. She then drew a small heart going into the machine and a large heart coming out. Again, she recorded on the T-chart and erased to make room for her next shape. (See Figure 13–1.)

At another table, Jared was working with the same idea but didn't draw a machine. He had a large T-chart taking up most of his paper. He was recording small shapes on the left and slightly larger shapes on the right.

I felt a tap on my elbow and turned to see Cameron standing behind me. "Can I use numbers in my machine?" he asked. I told him he could, curious to see what he would do.

Paulo had a different approach. He had drawn his own version of a machine, taking up most of his paper. When I walked by, he was making grinding noises as he decorated his drawing. "I'm going to come back in one minute and you need to be finished drawing your machine," I commented,

FIGURE 13–1 Latasha made little shapes into big shapes. She drew each shape going into and coming out of the machine, erasing what she had drawn before drawing the next pair of shapes.

realizing that the imagery of the machine was much more interesting to Paulo than what went in and came out. When I came back to Paulo's table, he was still drawing. When he saw me he stopped and drew a small triangle going into his machine.

"What's going to come out?" I asked.

"A *big* triangle," he said, drawing a large triangle on the right side of his paper.

"What's next?" I prompted.

"I have another idea," he responded, turning his paper over. "But I have to make a different machine."

I knelt down next to Paulo and said quietly and firmly, "OK, but don't take too much time drawing a machine. I'm more interested in how you think about things that go into and come out of the machine. Also, you need to draw a T-chart to go with your new machine. I'm going to come back soon and check on your progress." My past experiences with Paulo had taught me to let him do things his own way for a while before insisting he follow my directions.

I continued to circulate, seeing that most students were busily working on their T-charts. Peter had a small machine in the middle of his paper and was working on his third T-chart when I walked by. As Latasha had done, Peter carefully drew each item that went into the machine and came out of the machine before recording on the T-chart.

I checked to see what Cameron had done and was surprised to see that he had written two very different T-charts, using numbers on both. I asked him to tell me about what he'd done and he said that on the first chart he was adding three to each number. Referring to the second T-chart, he said, "This one is the numbers going diagonal," pointing to the 1–100 chart on the wall near his desk. Not sure what he meant, I asked him to show me on the 1–100 chart. He walked to the chart and pointed to the 9. "See, it's diagonal," he said, moving his finger diagonally down and left to the 18. He showed me several more examples—27 to 36, 45 to 54, and so on—each time showing how he got the second number by moving down and to the left diagonally. I noticed later that he had made a few errors on his T-chart, but I felt these were careless errors. I was confident that he understood the concept that the machine did the same thing to each number put in. (See Figure 13–2.)

When most of the students had made several entries on their T-charts, I interrupted them and announced, "When you're done, write a sentence that describes what your machine is doing." Latasha wrote: *It's turning the little shapes into big shapes.* Jared wrote: *little shapes go in big come out.* Amy wrote: *The rule is blank color.* (See Figure 13–3.) Richard wrote: *It makes things huge.* Cameron wrote *adding 3 to the number* for his first T-chart and *going diangle in numbers* for his second chart.

As students finished writing, I asked them to share their papers at their tables. Then I asked for volunteers to share their work with the class. In turn, Amy, Shivani, and Jared brought their papers to the front of the room, read their sentences, and held up their papers for the class to see. After each person presented we clapped. With many eager hands still in the air, the bell rang for recess and I assured the class that there would be more time to share soon. Figure 13–4 shows one other student's rule.

FIGURE 13–2

Cameron chose to use numbers and wrote two T-charts. In his first, he added three to the number that went in. In the second, he moved from the input number diagonally down to the left on the 1–100 wall chart to get the output.

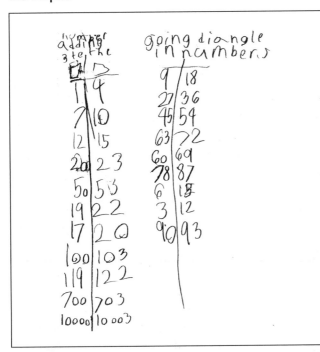

FIGURE 13–3

For her rule, Amy started with blank shapes and then colored them in.

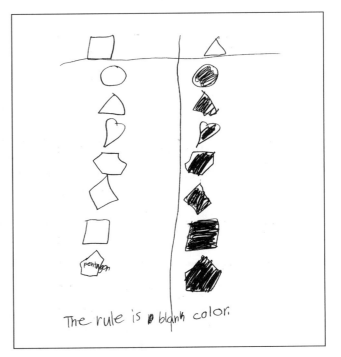

FIGURE 13–4 For each shape that Lisa put into her magic machine, two of the same shape came out.

Day 2

I gathered the class on the carpet in the front of the room and began, "Today we're going to make machines again." I drew a machine on the board as I had done the day before.

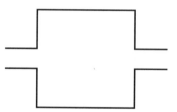

"But we're going to do something a little bit different today," I continued. "Yesterday, Cameron asked me if he could put numbers into his machine and today, instead of putting shapes into the machine, we're all going to put numbers in."

If Cameron hadn't asked to put numbers into his machine the day before, I would have made the suggestion now and then introduced the rule that Cameron had used. In your class, feel free to introduce Cameron's idea as one from a boy in another second-grade class.

"Let's take a look at what Cameron did and see if you can figure out what his machine was doing," I said. I drew a T-chart on the board and listed the first two pairs of numbers from Cameron's first T-chart As I wrote the numbers, I referred to them as going into and coming out of the machine, saying, "He put in a one and out came a four. He put in a seven and out came a ten." I continued in this way until I had listed four pairs of numbers.

In	Out
1	4
7	10
12	15
20	23

Next I said, "Let's see, to get from one to four I wonder what the machine did?" Not stopping for answers, I continued, "To get from seven to ten, it must have done the same thing . . . " Pausing for a moment to let students think, I pointed to the 12 and the 15, "And it did the same thing here." I turned to the class and said, "Raise your hand if you know what the machine is doing." I asked for a show of hands at this point to see how many students were with me. I wanted them to have a chance to formulate their own theory of what the machine was doing from looking at the T-chart. I tried to find the delicate balance between leading them to discover the relationship between the numbers and giving it away. It's important to be explicit that the relationship between the numbers in the columns on a T-chart is the same for all numbers that go in.

"Now try your idea of what the machine is doing on the next pair of numbers," I said, pointing first to the 20 and then to the 23 next to it. "You put in twenty, the machine does something, and out comes twenty-three. Raise your hand if you have an idea about what the machine did for the other numbers that also works for twenty and twenty-three." I said this to encourage students to convince themselves that their ideas were correct or incorrect based on the information they had in front of them. So often students look to teachers to validate their own thinking, and it's important to give them ways to rely on making sense for themselves.

I still didn't ask any of the children to explain their ideas. I wanted to give all of them some more time to think, so I said, "Let's try one more." I wrote 50 in the left column. "Next Cameron put fifty into his machine. What number do you think came out?" Many hands went up and I asked students to share what they thought with someone near them. I then asked them to whisper their answer on the count of three, and the students whispered loudly, "Fifty-three!" I recorded 53 on the T-chart.

In	Out
1	4
7	10
12	15
20	23
50	53

I asked Cameron if we could borrow his machine's rule and try some numbers of our own. He nodded in agreement and I asked, "What if we put three into the machine? Everybody whisper."

The class responded, "Six!" I continued asking what would happen if we put in 60, 160, and 800 into the machine. This class was interested in large numbers, but in other classes, I would choose different input numbers for the students to think about, deciding what was appropriate to support the children's mental arithmetic skills. Each time, I listed the pairs of numbers on the chart as the class answered.

In	Out
1	4
7	10
12	15
20	23
50	53
3	6
60	63
160	163
800	803

Confident that most of the students saw the relationship between the numbers in the left and right columns of the T-chart, I asked who would like to describe the rule that the machine was following.

"You add three to the number," Richard said.

"It's counting by threes," Paulo added.

"I just went up three," Latasha said.

I looked at Cameron for verification. "I did plus three," he said.

To do a little more work with this particular relationship before moving on, I asked, "Who would like to choose a number to put into Cameron's machine?" All hands were up. Before I called on anyone, I said, "When I call on you, tell us just the number that goes in. Then, after we've all thought about it, you can tell us what number comes out. We'll show a thumb up if we agree. Now think quietly for a minute about what number you'd like to put in and what number will come out." I gave the children a bit more time to think and then called on Richard.

"Three thousand," he said with a grin. After a moment, I had him reveal what number came out of the machine. "Three thousand three," he said, and the others showed thumbs up. I recorded on the T-chart. I continued in this way, giving several more children the chance to give input and output numbers.

In	Out
1	4
7	10
12	15
20	23
50	53
60	63
3	6
160	163
800	803
3000	3003
100	103
1000	1003

Another Function Rule   "Now I'm going to change the settings on the machine. On the T-chart, I'm going to write a few numbers that went in and came out. Raise your hand when you think you know the new rule," I said, drawing a new T-chart and recording four pairs of numbers, choosing the rule of doubling the input number.

In	Out
1	2
2	4
3	6
4	8

Most of the students had a hand up. "What do you notice?" I asked.

"The next number after is in order," Paulo said.

"Where do you see that?" I asked, curious to understand what he was noticing.

"One, two, three, four," he said, referring to the left column of the chart.

"Yes, you're right," I responded. "That's interesting, but I don't have to write those numbers in order. I could put in nine, for example." I wrote *9* in the left column. "This time nine goes into the machine and eighteen comes out." I wrote *18* in the right column. I chose a number out of order to push students to think about the relationship across the columns in the T-chart, between pairs of input and output numbers.

"Think about what's happening to the numbers on the left to make them turn into the numbers on the right," I said. "I'm going to give you one more example and then we'll talk about what the machine is doing." I wrote *10* in the left column. "If I write ten on this side, then I have to write twenty on the right side," I said, changing my terminology slightly and then recording *20*.

In	Out
1	2
2	4
3	6
4	8
9	18
10	20

"Ten plus ten is twenty," Peter said excitedly.

"Does that work for the other pairs of numbers?" I asked. "One plus one is . . . ?" I said, pausing.

"Two plus two is . . . ?"

"What if we put one hundred here?" I said, writing it in the left column.

"Two hundred!" the children responded loudly.

"What about if the number five goes into the machine?" I said, continuing to list numbers on the T-chart.

"Ten!" came the response.

"What about seven?" I asked.

After a brief pause, some children answered fourteen, but many weren't quite as sure of this double.

In	Out
1	2
2	4
3	6
4	8
9	18
10	20
100	200
5	10
7	14

"Who can describe what the machine is doing?" I asked.

"It doubles," Marie answered.

"It adds itself," Amy added.

I felt confident that the class saw the relationship between the sets of numbers. I moved on to give directions for a class assignment. "Now it's your turn to think of your own rule for a machine using numbers. Make a T-chart to show what numbers go in and what numbers come out. When you're done, write a sentence that tells what your rule is."

Observing the Students   The children got to work much as they had the day before. Some drew machines first; others made large T-charts in the middle of their papers. I was particularly pleased to see Paulo immediately draw a large T-chart in the middle of his paper and begin writing numbers. On the left side he wrote *6 + 6*, matched with *12* in the right column. Next he wrote *4 + 4* and *8*.

Latasha diligently wrote each number on the left side of her machine drawing and then listed it on her T-chart. She then figured out the corresponding number, wrote it on the right side of the machine, and then recorded it on the T-chart. Her numbers were 40 and 80, 50 and 100, and 60 and 120. She wrote: *I am adding the same number I put in.*

Jared wrote: *My rule is when 5 10 comes out.* I said to him, "I see that when you started with five, ten came out. What about the other numbers you put in?" I pointed to the left-hand column of his T-chart. "What did you do to each of those numbers?" I was pushing Jared to make a more general description of what he'd done. He began another sentence and I watched as he wrote: *I am adding 5.*

"That helps me understand what you did," I said. For input numbers, Jared had used only multiples of five, and I now asked him, "What about if I wanted to put a different number in the machine? What about if I put a three in? What number would come out?" I was curious to find out if Jared understood that he could put any number in the input column. I worried that he thought that the adding five rule applied also, in some way, to the numbers that went into the machine.

Jared thought for a moment and then said, "Eight would come out. Three and five more is eight." Satisfied that he wasn't confused, I left him to continue working. (See Figure 13–5.)

FIGURE 13–5 Jared's pattern was to add five to the numbers that go into the machine. He chose multiples of five as input numbers, as they were easier for him to use to figure out the outputs.

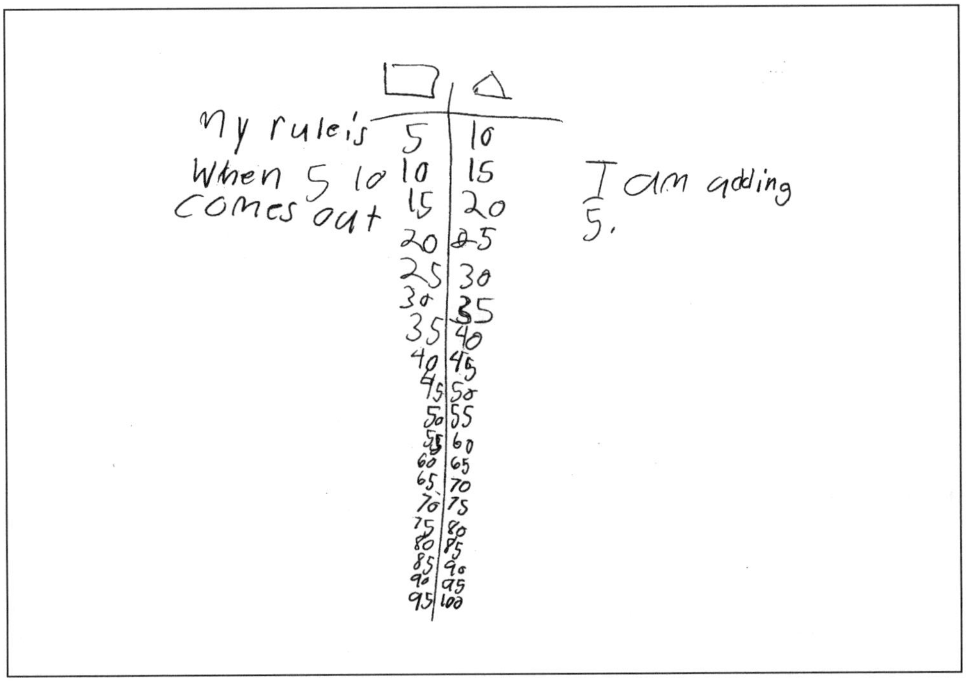

Meanwhile, I'd noticed Richard working intently with a number line on his desk. I looked at his paper and he'd written a line down the middle and four pairs of numbers—5 and 2, 10 and 7, 13 and 10, 9 and 6. Not wanting to disrupt his concentration too much, I said quietly, "Make sure you get a chance to write about what you're doing before it's time to clean up." Later I looked at his paper. He'd written: *When one number comes out it takes away three.* He'd also recorded two more pairs of numbers—20 and 17 and 30 and 27.

Nearby, Cameron was adding sixty to each of the numbers he listed on the left side of his T-chart. After a while he turned his paper over and worked with adding seventy, listing pairs of numbers such as 0 and 70 and 20 and 90. (See Figure 13–6.)

Amy made two different machines with corresponding T-charts. Underneath one she wrote: *counting by twos.* Underneath the other she wrote: *The rule is double double and then add.* (See Figure 13–7.)

A few minutes before it was time to clean up, I interrupted the students and asked them to share their work with the person sitting next to them. "Mine's hard," said Richard with a shy smile.

Figure 13–8 shows one other student's rule.

FIGURE 13–6

The numbers in both columns on Cameron's T-chart reflect his interest in large numbers.

100	160
300	3060
40000	40060
50	110
70	130
60	120
150	210
40	100

adding 60 to the number.

FIGURE 13–7

Amy drew an elaborate, mazelike machine. She chose input numbers at random and doubled each. She saw the pattern as adding the numbers to themselves.

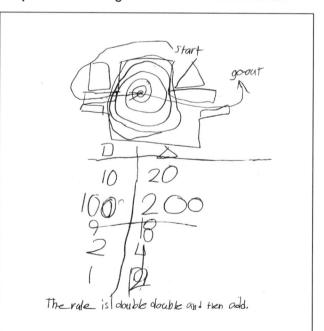

start
go out

10	20
100	200
9	18
2	4
1	2

The rule is double double and then add.

FIGURE 13-8 Marie added two to the input numbers. In her description, she referred to the pattern as a skip-counting pattern. She maintained the pattern for both input and output numbers.

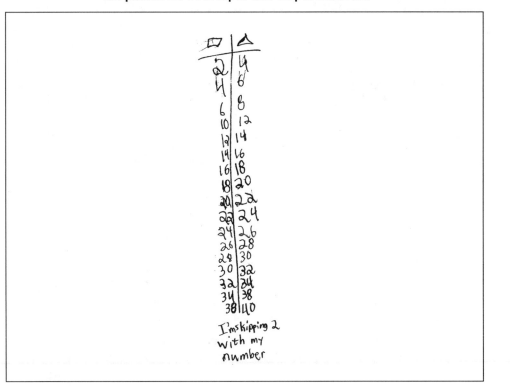

Extensions

Pair children with new partners. Have one present his or her T-chart and the other try to guess the rule. Then have them switch roles. You can also have children present their T-charts to the entire class and have the class try to figure out the rule.

14

Dot Cards

Version 2

OVERVIEW

U sing small blank cards with a line dividing each in half, children first figure out all the different ways to draw ten dots on cards with some on each side of the line. They then repeat the exploration for other numbers of dots, from six to thirteen. Once they have made sets of cards for different numbers of dots, children play the game of *Dot Cards*, comparing the numbers of dots on pairs of cards and recording number sentences using >, <, or =. Children also investigate the pattern of how many different cards are possible for different numbers.

BACKGROUND

The game of *Dot Cards* gives children experience decomposing numbers into two addends, comparing quantities, and writing number sentences using =, >, and <. The activity supports children's arithmetic learning while emphasizing the important ideas of equality and inequality. The lesson is similar to Chapter 11, "*Two Handfuls*," but presents the ideas in a new context and, therefore, provides a fresh experience for the students.

In this lesson, children explore different ways to represent numbers as the sum of two addends and find all of the possible combinations to do so for different numbers. They begin with the number ten and, as a class, find out that there are eleven possibilities—10 + 0, 9 + 1, 8 + 2, 7 + 3, and so on. After exploring other numbers on their own, children investigate the relationship between a number and the number of combinations of two addends that represent it. The pattern reveals that the number of possibilities is always one more than the number being investigated. This relationship is an example of a function, a fundamental notion in algebra. While I don't define the relationship as a function for the children or expect the children to represent the relationship symbolically, the investigation adds to children's foundation of algebraic understanding.

The lesson as described was taught to second graders and is appropriate for both first and second graders. For kindergarten children, making dot cards for smaller numbers, as suggested in Chapter 4, "*Dot Cards, Version 1*," is more appropriate. For first graders, skip the investigation presented for Day

3 about the number of different cards possible for different numbers. Instead, give the children more time to work on making their own dot cards for other numbers, and then teach them how to use their cards to play the game.

VOCABULARY

equals, fewer, greater, less, more, pattern

MATERIALS

- $8\frac{1}{2}$-by-11-inch card stock, 3–4 sheets per student, each cut into eighths to make $4\frac{1}{4}$-by $2\frac{3}{4}$-inch cards

TIME

- four class periods, plus additional time for playing

Day 1

The Lesson

The children spilled into the classroom, full of stories from the weekend. I called for their attention and told them that there would be time for them to share their news later. "This week we're going to learn a new math game, called *Dot Cards*," I began. "But before we play the game we have to make the dot cards. You're going to use cards that look like this." I had cut $8\frac{1}{2}$-by-11-inch card stock into eighths so that I had a stack of $4\frac{1}{4}$-by $2\frac{3}{4}$-inch cards, and I had drawn a dark line down the middle of each.

"These cards are too small for you to see from your seats, so I'm going to draw a card on the board," I said, drawing a rectangle with a line down the middle large enough for the entire class to see.

"In order to play the game we need lots of cards with different numbers of dots on them. Today you'll start by making cards with ten dots on them, and you'll try to find all the different ways to arrange the dots. For example, when you make a dot card you can put some dots on each side of the line or all of the dots together on the left or the right," I said, pointing to my sample card on the board. "Think quietly to yourself how you could arrange exactly ten dots on a card that looks like this. After you think of one way, try to think of another. I'll tell you when quiet thinking time is over and you can talk to the people at your table." I often give students time to think quietly before discussing problems in pairs or groups. Students approach problems in a variety of ways, and I want to make sure that each individual has a chance to begin formulating ideas before being introduced to other perspectives. This quiet thinking time gives students who often are eager to answer first a chance to reflect a bit more before speaking. Also, students who need more time before speaking aren't put on the spot to communicate before they're ready.

After a moment, I asked students to share their ideas with their group members. After a minute of sharing, I interrupted and asked, "Who would like to share with the class the solutions you discussed in your group?" I purposely asked for solutions from the group rather than from individuals, hoping to build a culture of shared ideas rather than proprietary information.

"We all said to put five on one side and five on the other," Paulo said.

"We got that, too," Bethany said from another table.

"Great! You both had the same good idea," I responded, and drew fives dots as Paulo had suggested on each side of my sample card. I didn't ask the children how they visualized the dots, but used a different pattern on each side to model for the children that there wasn't one correct way to display them. Also, I wrote a *5* on each side of the card.

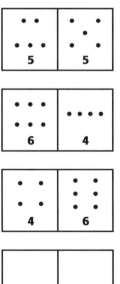

"I drew the dots and then wrote the number of dots that are on each side of the card," I explained. "You'll do the same when you make your cards—draw the dots and write the numbers."

I drew another blank card on the board and asked for another arrangement of ten dots. Peter suggested six and four. I followed his suggestion, drawing dots and recording the numbers. Then I drew another blank card. Next Marie suggested four and six. "I'm just turning the numbers around," she explained. I recorded her idea and drew another blank card.

Amy waved her hand wildly. "*Ten* plus *zero*! We forgot that one," she exclaimed.

"And zero plus ten," Bethany added. I recorded both of these.

"Four and six," Nadia then suggested. I knew that I had already recorded that arrangement, but I wanted to acknowledge Nadia's thinking. "Yes, that's a good idea, Nadia, but I think I've already drawn that one. Let's see if we can find it on the board." I gave the students a moment and several spotted the card quickly. "So I don't have to draw that one again. I'm glad you suggested it, Nadia. It's a good reminder to check when you're making your cards to be sure that you're not making duplicates."

"Then two and eight," Nadia said, making a suggestion for a card I hadn't yet recorded. I nodded and added it to the board.

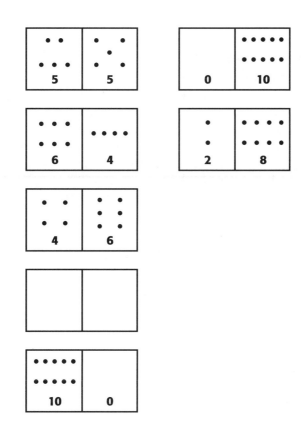

Soon each new suggestion was a repeat of something already on the board. I asked the children to show a thumb up if they thought they had found all the ways to arrange ten dots. About half the class agreed, while the other half either disagreed with a thumb down or held a thumb sideways to show that they weren't sure.

"I think I have a way that could help us figure out if we've found all the ways to make dot cards with exactly ten dots," I said, drawing a large T-chart on the board. "This is a T-chart," I reminded the class. I traced over the T again and explained, "See how it looks like a giant T? I'll show you how to record the dot cards on the T-chart just using numbers, and that can help us see if we have them all." Above each column I drew two small blank dot cards. I shaded in the left side of the card at the top of the left column and the right side of the card on the top of the right column.

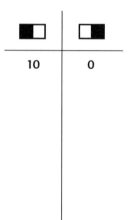

"This will help us remember which side the dots are on. We're always going to write the number of dots on the left side of the card first," I said, pointing to the shaded part of the card at the top of the left column. "Then we'll write the number of dots on the right side in the right column," I added, pointing to the shaded part of the card at the top of the right column.

I then said, "I'm going to start with ten and zero." I wrote *10* in the left column of the T-chart and *0* in the right column. I chose this card because I planned to list all of the cards with the numbers in order. I could have begun with zero and ten, but since children often find it easier to think of combinations with the larger number first, I began with ten and zero.

"I'm going to put a check next to this card so we know we've used this one," I said, referring to the drawing of the ten and zero card on the board. "After ten and zero I'm going to put nine and . . . " I paused, waiting for the class to answer, wrote *9* and *1* on the T-chart, and put a check next to the corresponding card drawn on the board.

■□	□■
10	0
9	1

"Which card do you think we should use next?" I asked, hoping that the students had enough information to see the pattern.

"Eight and two," Reginald announced.

"Why did you pick that one?" I asked.

"'Cause that's the next one in order—ten, nine, eight," he said, pointing to the numbers in the left column on the T-chart.

After recording the next four cards, I asked students what they noticed about the numbers on the chart.

■□	□■
10	0
9	1
8	2
7	3
6	4
5	5
4	6

"It's a pattern," Bethany said, "Zero, one, two, three, four, five, six."

"Can anyone describe the pattern on the left column of the T-chart?" I asked.

"It's, like, backwards. I think there could be a blastoff," Peter said mischievously.

"Let's see if we can use these number patterns to help figure out the numbers that come next," I said. "Count with me: ten, nine, eight, seven, six, five, four . . . ," I paused, giving the class a chance to say the next number in the sequence.

"Three!" most of the students answered. I wrote *3* in the left column.

"And how many dots would be on the right side of the card if it had three dots on the left side?" I asked, pointing to the space in the right column.

"Seven is with that," Richard said.

"What made you choose seven?" I asked, curious to see if he used the pattern.

"Three and seven is ten; it's that one," he said, pointing to one of the cards I had drawn on the board.

"That's interesting. Do you think each of these pairs of numbers will add up to ten?" I asked the class. Although this may seem obvious, it's important to make the relationship explicit. One of the goals of this lesson is to present mathematical information in various ways, and I'm careful not to assume that students are making connections just because those connections are clear to me.

"Let's check," I said, pointing to and talking about each pair of numbers on the T-chart. I modeled several ways of checking—counting on, drawing tally marks, using Snap Cubes, referring to the 1–100 chart, and using fingers. Although many students "just know" many of these combinations, I push them to give evidence to explain what they know. Ultimately, I want all my students to "just know" their basic facts, but I also want them to have strategies to use when they forget, and ways to explain how they know what they know.

After confirming that each pair of numbers we had listed so far added up to ten, I commented, "Let's see if three and seven follow the patterns of the numbers in the columns." Again we said the sequence of numbers on the left side of the chart together and confirmed that three came next. We did the same thing with the sequence of numbers on the right side of the chart, agreeing that seven fit the pattern. I wrote 7 in the right column and put a check mark next to the corresponding dot card. After recording 2 and 8, 1 and 9, and 0 and 10, I asked for a show of hands of who thought we had listed all of the cards we had made. About half the students raised their hands.

"Let's check one more time to make sure we listed all the cards we found," I said, wanting again to connect the information on the T-chart with the dot cards. We confirmed one by one that each pair of numbers on the chart corresponded to a dot card that had been checked off.

■□	□■
10	0
9	1
8	2
7	3
6	4
5	5
4	6
3	7
2	8
1	9
0	10

"It looks like we recorded all of them," I said. "Do you think there are any more dot cards that we forgot to make?" I asked, not sure if students felt the T-chart was convincing evidence of having found all the combinations. No hands went up so I decided to leave this idea for now and move on.

"How many different dot cards did we make that have exactly ten dots?" I asked. Students began quietly counting the cards on the board.

"Let's count together," I suggested. We found that there were eleven cards. I then suggested that we count the pairs of numbers on the T-chart to make sure that we had eleven there too. We did.

"We've found eleven ways to make cards with ten dots. I'm going to write that down so that we remember what we found out," I said, writing *10 dots—11 cards* below the middle of a piece of construction paper. Later I would record the number of cards for other numbers of dots and ask the children to see what pattern they noticed. Therefore, I left room on the construction paper to record smaller numbers of dots above.

10 dots—11 cards

"Now it's your turn to make your own set of ten-dot cards," I said, holding up the blank cards. "I'd like you to make all the different cards with ten dots that you can. I'd also like you to make a T-chart to help you check to see if you've found them all. You may work with a partner at your table, but I'd like you each to make your own set of cards and your own T-chart. Please put your initials on the back of each of your dot cards."

The children were eager to get started, but I posed a question before distributing the blank cards. "How many blank cards should I put on your table for each person?" I was curious to see if anyone would make a connection to the information we were just discussing.

"Maybe eleven?" Marie said. No one else offered an opinion, so I distributed the cards and the students got to work. In addition to the blank cards, I distributed paper for their T-charts. I left all of the information on the board. From past experience, I've learned that most children approach the project in their own ways without copying what's recorded on the board, while others need to refer to the board for help.

Observing the Students   Peter began by making a card with five dots on each side, meticulously positioning the dots. He then made a card for ten and zero dots, followed by a card for zero and ten dots. I watched as he stopped, apparently stumped as what to do next. I was surprised that with all the information on the board he still was stuck, but I decided not to intervene. Finally, he took a new card and made a card with four and six dots. I realized that rather than being stuck, he was just thinking. Although I was curious to know what he was thinking about, Peter wasn't usually so focused, and I decided not to disturb his concentration. (See Figure 14–1.)

I noticed Reginald had turned his cards vertically and was drawing large circles for dots. This was fine with me. I was concerned more with the mathematical correctness than the appearance of the cards.

At a different table, I saw Lisa placing each finished card in a row on her desk. She appeared to be making her cards in the order they were listed on the T-chart. When she finished making her cards, she counted them and began making her T-chart.

FIGURE 14-1 Peter listed all of the possible cards for ten dots.

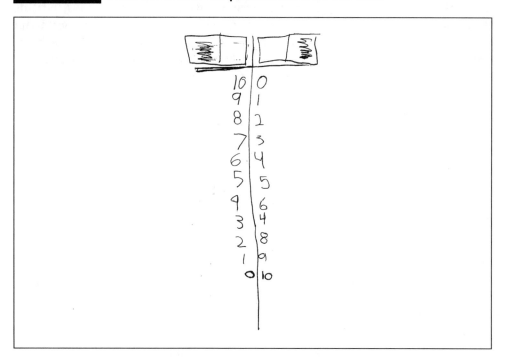

Jared, on the other hand, made his T-chart first, checking the board as he went. Then he made his cards.

Navjot created her T-chart as she made her cards, recording a pair of numbers each time she completed a card. She began with nine and one, then five and five, and continued in a random order. By the end of the period she had made seven cards and listed the numbers on her T-chart. (See Figure 14–2.)

FIGURE 14-2 Navjot recorded each card as she completed drawing the dots, making the cards in random order. By the end of the period, she had made seven of the eleven possibilities.

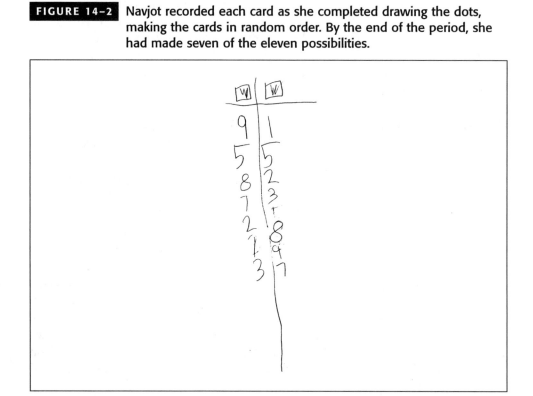

At one point Nadia came to me and asked for another piece of paper. "I ran out of room on my T-chart," she told me. I followed her to her desk and saw that she had placed each of her finished cards on the T-chart with the line on the card placed to match the line on the chart and the numbers on the cards creating the entries on the chart. I hadn't thought to connect the line in the middle of the dot cards with the line in the middle of the T-chart, and I was pleased that she had clearly made the connection between the cards and the T-chart. I gave her another piece of paper and she continued her T-chart. When it was time to clean up, Nadia was almost finished making her cards, but I realized that she hadn't had time to record what she did on the paper underneath her cards. I was glad that I had observed her working, as there was no record of the method she had used.

Not everyone had completed his or her set of dot cards, and I assured the children that they would have time the next day to finish. I passed out a paper clip to each student and they clipped their cards to their T-charts.

Figure 14–3 shows one more student's T-chart.

FIGURE 14–3 Travis drew lines to show which numbers in the left column matched which numbers in the right column. He was missing only one card, the one with zero dots on the left and ten on the right.

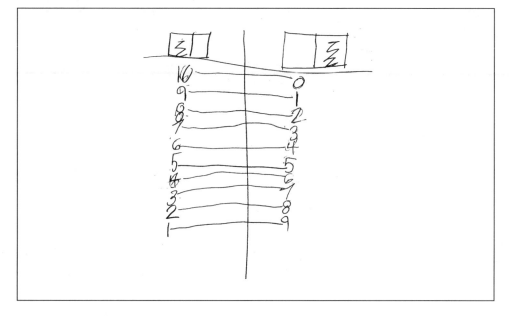

Day 2

My plan for the second day was for students to make cards with other numbers of dots on them. I began class by asking the students what they remembered from the day before.

"We made cards with dots," Peter said.

"Cards with *ten* dots and the chart thingy," Reginald added.

"I didn't get to finish," Bethany said.

"Well, today you'll get to finish your cards with ten dots and you'll also make a set of cards with six dots," I said, leading into the lesson. Working with ten dots first made sense to me because we had done a great deal of work on numbers that add to ten, so the children were familiar with the combinations. I chose six dots for their next set because it was the smallest number of dots for which they would make cards, and I felt that all of the students would be successful finding the combinations of six.

"Yesterday we decided that there were eleven ways to make dot cards with ten dots," I said, pointing to the poster I'd started the day before. "How many ways do you think there are to make dot cards with exactly six dots?" I asked.

"Maybe ten," Beatriz suggested.

"Twenty?" Paulo asked.

"I think there's seven ways," Cameron sad quietly.

"Remember your predictions," I said. "We'll talk about this again after we find all the ways to arrange six dots."

I repeated the process from the previous day, first drawing blank cards on the board and taking students' suggestions for how many dots to put on each side. Again, I made a T-chart and together we listed the numbers in order from 6 and 0 to 0 and 6, checking off each card as we went. After counting how many cards we'd made and checking the T-chart to confirm that we had the same number of combinations, I recorded *6 dots—7 cards* on the poster I'd started the day before, leaving room for other entries between six and ten dots and for entries above six dots. I also labeled the poster *How Many Cards?*

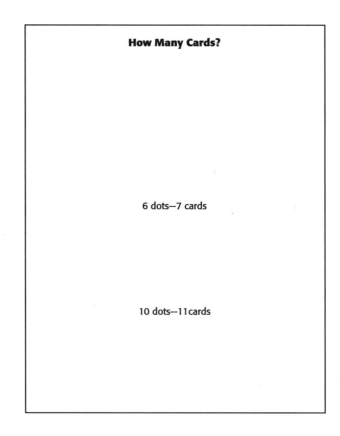

How Many Cards?

6 dots—7 cards

10 dots—11 cards

"Today you'll finish your cards with ten dots and then you'll make a set of cards with exactly six dots on each. When you're finished, you can pick the next number of dots you'd like to work on. I'm going to list your choices on the poster." I filled in the poster with the numbers missing between six and ten and extended it to thirteen dots.

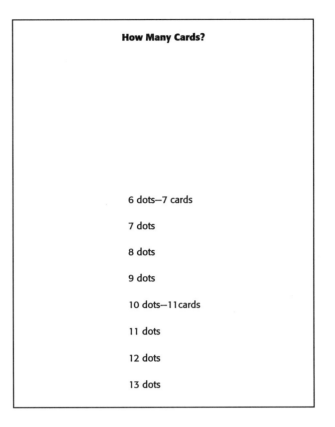

How Many Cards?

6 dots—7 cards

7 dots

8 dots

9 dots

10 dots—11 cards

11 dots

12 dots

13 dots

"Can I make cards with fourteen dots?" Peter asked with a gleam in his eye.

"You'll have time later to pick different numbers, but these are your choices for today," I responded, pointing to the chart. On the board I wrote the directions for work time, then I reviewed them aloud.

Finish making dot cards and a T-chart for 10 dots.
Make dot cards and a T-chart for 6 dots.
Choose another number from the poster and make dot cards and a T-chart.
  Your choices are: 7 dots, 8 dots, 9 dots, 11 dots, 12 dots, 13 dots.

I placed a stack of blank dot cards on each table along with several sheets of blank paper. I directed the students' attention to a table by the door where they could find extra blank paper, dot cards, and unfinished work from the day before. Several students got up to retrieve their work, while the rest began working on dot cards with six dots. After checking that everyone had begun working, I erased the work we'd done together with six dots, leaving only the written directions and the How Many Cards? poster. Since six was a smaller number and they had the experience from the day before, I wanted to see what they would do without the support of the work we had done on the board.

Observing the Students   As the students worked, I circulated, watching and listening. As he had done the day before, Jared began by making his T-chart first and then his dot cards. Although the numbers on his T-chart were in order, he didn't make the cards in order. However, he did make a complete set. (See Figure 14–4.)

FIGURE 14–4   Jared correctly listed all the possible cards with seven dots on each.

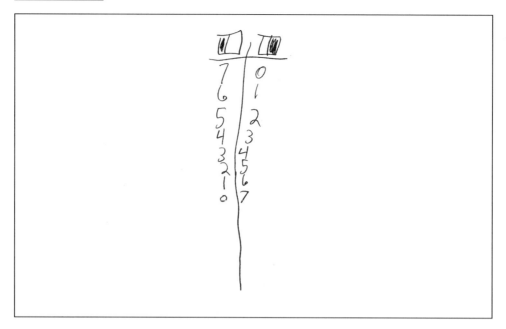

As Peter had done the day before, he began by recording the double in the middle of his chart, in this instance *3* and *3*. Then he wrote *6* and *0* at the top of the chart, followed by *0* and *6* at the bottom. He finished making all seven cards fairly quickly and completed the chart. I asked him to count how many cards he'd made and, on the back of his paper, write a sentence about his discovery. He counted and wrote: *There are 7 ways 2 make dot cards of 6.* I left him to think about what number of dots to work on next.

Latasha began her chart at the bottom of her paper, with *0* and *6*. She then made a dot card to match the numbers and continued the pattern up the chart, making a card after each entry. I asked Latasha why she'd started at the bottom of her paper and she said, "So I have room." Still curious, I moved on.

I found Navjot hunched over her desk, the thick lenses of her glasses inches from the card she was working on. I noticed the completed T-chart with the numbers listed in order, unlike her work the day before, and I wondered what had happened to cause her to put them in order. I also realized that she may have simply copied her chart from someone near her, and I made a note to try to be nearby when she began working on her next set of cards.

Next to Navjot, I noticed Marie had completed making cards for six dots and was working on a T-chart for eleven dots. She had written all the pairs of numbers in order, beginning with *11* and *0*. She was now busily drawing a tiny dot card next to each set of numbers. Her cards were a bit bigger than her numbers, so she drew a line to connect each picture with the corresponding numbers. (See Figure 14–5.)

By this time Myles had moved on to working on dot cards with thirteen dots. When he reached the bottom of his paper, he began a new column of numbers on each side and continued working. He finished his T-chart and then began making dot cards. First he wrote the numbers with the cards facing vertically, as Reginald had done the day before. Then, he drew the dots inside or around the numbers. (See Figure 14–6.)

Across the room, Reginald was also working on thirteen dots. He began by making a card with five dots on one side. Then he looked up at

FIGURE 14-5 Along with recording the numbers on a T-chart, Marie drew pictures of the dot cards she made.

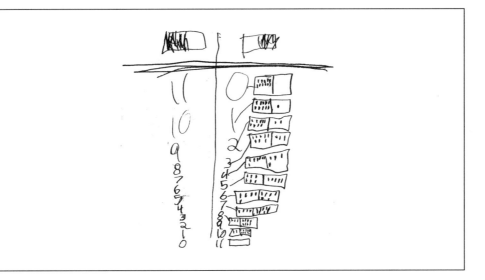

FIGURE 14-6 Myles recorded all the possible dot cards with thirteen dots. He ran out of room and had to make two columns on each side of his T-chart.

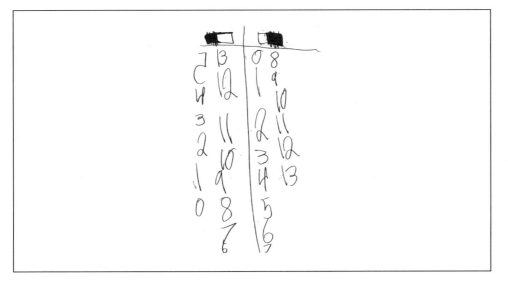

the calendar on the wall, pointed to the 5, and counted from five to thirteen, saying, "Five, six, seven, eight . . . ," as he pointed to the numbers on the calendar. When his finger was pointing at the 13, he stopped and drew eight dots on the other side of his card.

At that moment I felt a tug on my sleeve. I turned to see Bethany standing behind me. "I'm stuck," she said in a slightly pouty tone.

"Let's see what you've got so far," I said, and followed her back to her desk. On her paper she had drawn a T-chart and written *7* and *0*, *6* and *1*, and *5* and *2*. "It looks like you're working on seven dots," I said encouragingly. Bethany nodded in agreement. "Maybe the patterns can help us," I suggested. "Let's say the numbers you have in the left column out loud and see if they give us a clue."

Together we said, "Seven, six, five . . . "

After a pause, Bethany happily said, "Four!" and wrote *4* in the left column on her T-chart.

CHAPTER 16

Four in a Row

OVERVIEW

In this lesson, students investigate patterns in the coordinates for points arranged in horizontal and vertical lines and then, for an extension, in diagonal lines. The lesson not only gives students practice identifying ordered pairs for points and using them to locate points on a coordinate grid, but also engages students in looking for patterns. The lesson is appropriate after students have learned to use ordered pairs of numbers to plot points.

BACKGROUND

The prerequisite skill for this lesson is that students are able to plot points and also to identify the ordered pairs for points on a coordinate grid. The lesson is appropriate after students have learned to plot points and have had experience playing the game of *Tic-Tac-Toe* (see Chapter 5). The lesson as described was taught to second graders. The lesson is appropriate for second graders and some first graders, but not for kindergarten children. If you teach this lesson to first graders, it may be best for them to investigate only points in horizontal and vertical lines, not in diagonal lines as suggested in the "Extensions" section. For information about plotting points, see the "Background" section in Chapter 5.

VOCABULARY

diagonal, grid, horizontal, point, T-chart, vertical

MATERIALS

- *Tic-Tac-Toe Grid* worksheet, several per student (see Blackline Masters)
- optional: overhead transparency of *Tic-Tac-Toe Grid* worksheet

■ one class period, plus one period for the extension

The Lesson

After the children had played several games of *Tic-Tac-Toe*, I drew a T-chart on the board and listed four pairs of numbers:

□	△
1	2
2	2
3	2
4	2

I asked the children for their attention and said, "Here's a T-chart from someone who won a round of *Tic-Tac-Toe*. What do you notice?"

"The box numbers are counting," Bethany observed.

"It's all twos," Beatriz said, pointing to the right side of the T-chart.

"I'm going to show you a blank *Tic-Tac-Toe* game board," I said, turning on the overhead projector. (If you prefer, you can draw the grid on the chalkboard.) "See if you can imagine what this person's paper looked like. Where would the Xs or Os be?" I paused and there was no response. Realizing that this was a difficult request, I continued, "Who can read the numbers and tell us how to get to the first point?" Now several hands went up and I called on Richard.

"It's one to the box and two to the triangle," he said. Following his directions, I moved my pen the appropriate number of hops over and up and marked a point.

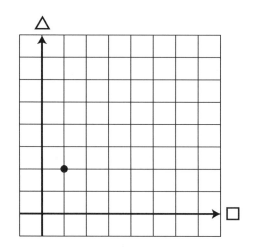

"I don't know if the person was using Xs or Os so I'm just going to mark a point. The next pair of numbers on the T-chart is two and two. Look at the grid and see if you can imagine where that point should be," I instructed, looking at the grid myself.

After a moment, I added, "Raise your hand if you think you know where the point for (two, two) goes. Let's count together and see." I placed my overhead pen at the origin and moved it as I counted aloud, "One, two toward the box and now one, two toward the triangle." I marked a point at (2, 2) and said, "Raise your hand if that is where you thought the point was going to be."

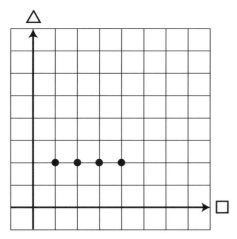

With two points on the grid, I said, "When we began, I told you that this was a T-chart from someone who won his or her game. What do you need in order to win?"

"It has to be four in a row, like Xs that way," Peter said, moving his hand horizontally.

"It can be diagonal, too," Reginald said, happy to have an opportunity to use his new favorite word.

"So where do you think the rest of the points on this person's paper should go?" I asked, directing their attention back to the grid.

"I think it's going to keep going in a row, because you said they won," said Latasha.

"This is called *horizontal*," I said, drawing a line on the board and writing the word *horizontal* next to it. "This is called *vertical*," I said, again drawing a line and labeling it with *vertical*. I didn't draw a diagonal line. Children often have difficulty remembering the difference between horizontal and vertical, and I didn't want to add the extra confusion of including diagonal as well.

"Raise your hand if you think this person's points are going to make a vertical line," I said, pointing to the grid and then to the vertical line on the board. No hands went up.

"Raise your hand if you think the four points will be in a horizontal line." I continued. Most hands went up.

"Let's find out," I said. "Who can tell me how to mark the next point?"

"Go three hops to the square," Eugene said, pausing. I followed his direction and stopped.

"Now two up again. They're all two up," Eugene said, happy to have a chance to share his observation. I followed his direction and made a third point on the grid.

"Now everyone quietly look at the last pair of numbers on this winning T-chart and think about where the fourth point is going to be," I said, pausing. After a few seconds I asked the class to count with me as I marked a point for (4, 2), the last pair on the T-chart.

□	△
3	2
3	3
3	4
3	5

"What do you notice about these four points?" I asked.

"They're horizontal?" Lisa said tentatively.

"Give me a thumbs up if you agree with Lisa that the points are in a horizontal row," I said. Everyone's thumb went up. Curious to see what else they were thinking, I asked, "What else do you notice?"

"They're kind of down at the bottom," Jared said.

"It's going one, two, three, four," Beatriz said, pointing to the points in order as she spoke.

No other student had a comment. I turned off the overhead projector and drew a new T-chart next to the one we'd just discussed. "This T-chart is from a different person who also won a game of *Tic-Tac-Toe*," I said, and then added, pointing to the numbers, "What do you notice about this T-chart?"

"There's numbers in order," Nadia said.

"It's got all threes on that side," Myles said excitedly.

"Where are the numbers all the same, on the box side or the triangle side?" I asked.

"The box side," several voices answered.

"What about the other T-chart we looked at," I said, pointing to it. "Which side had all the same number?"

"All the twos are on the triangle side," Cameron said.

"Hmm, and on this new T-chart, the square column has all threes. I wonder if that will help us figure out what the points are going to look like?" I pondered. Having wiped the first four points off the grid, I turned on the overhead projector and asked the students to think about where the points for the numbers on the new T-chart would be. Again we located the points one by one, discussing observations as we went. After plotting all four points, everyone agreed that they made a vertical line.

A Class Assignment   "Now it's your turn to mark four points in a row on your own paper, either horizontally or vertically. You'll do this as if you're playing *Tic-Tac-Toe* and you just won!" I said enthusiastically, then added,

"You can decide if you want to use Xs or Os or just mark four points to show how you won your game." I distributed blank game grids and an excited hum rose from the class as the children discussed how they were going to win their games. "Make sure to write down your moves on a T-chart. And when you're done, please write some sentences about what you notice."

Observing the Students   I watched Amy mark four Xs in a horizontal line near the top of her paper. She then began counting to figure out the numbers to record on her T-chart. I was fascinated to observe that she didn't list the coordinates in order. First she counted to the point (3, 6) and recorded, then she counted to the point (1, 6) and recorded. Watching this made me realize that while Amy had drawn the Xs in order from left to right, she didn't see the value in recording the points in order. After finishing her T-chart, Amy wrote: *I notice that it is going the same in the △ side because I am going horozontal and up high.* I handed Amy another grid and asked if she could show how she could win the game with points going vertically. She smiled and got to work. This time she listed the pairs in order from top to bottom.

Jared also completed two papers, one with points going horizontally and the other with points going vertically. On his first paper he wrote: *I notest that I got 4 in a horozontal line. I notest that all of my first numbers are in orter. I notest that all of my second number are 6.* (See Figure 16–1.) On his second paper he wrote: *I notest that all my fist numbers are 4. I notest that I got 4 in a vertical line. I notest my second numbers are in orter.*

Latasha also finished two papers. Like Amy, she did not list the numbers on her first paper in order. Her observations about her horizontal points were: *The numbers that are going tords the trangle are the same numbers. The numbers that are going tords the square are different.* On her second paper, with points arranged vertically, she listed the points in order and wrote: *The numbers that are going tords the triangle are going backwards. The numbers that are going tords the square are the same.* (See Figure 16–2.)

FIGURE 16–1   On his first paper, Jared marked four points in a horizontal row and wrote three sentences about what he noticed.

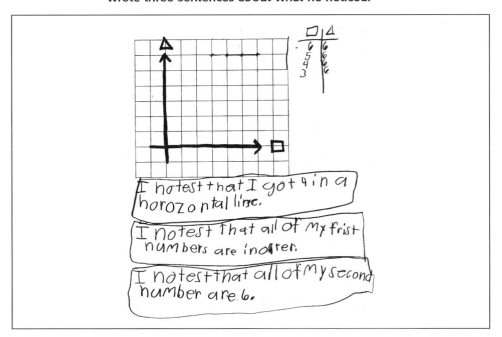

FIGURE 16-2 Latasha marked her four Xs vertically and explained that the numbers going toward the triangle were decreasing while the numbers going toward the box remained the same.

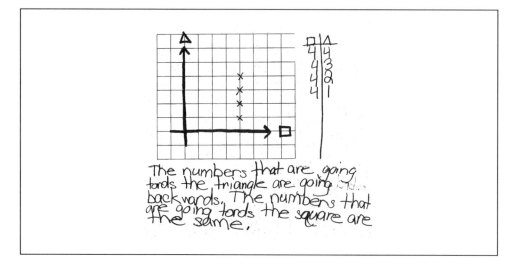

Richard made a row of points on the vertical axis. He wrote: *I got 4 in a row by counting down. And my ▢ side has all 0 and my △ side is counting down.* (See Figure 16-3.) Eugene made a horizontal row and wrote: *I one by 3 3 4 3 5 3 6 3 I thick it is a pater* [pattern] *because three and for and five and six make a pater.*

A few minutes before the period was over, I interrupted the class and asked for a show of hands of who'd made a horizontal row of points on their paper. About half of the students raised a hand. I then asked for a show of hands for those who'd made a vertical row. Again, about half raised a hand. As I began giving directions for cleaning up, Amy waved her hand at me frantically. I walked over to her to see what was so pressing. In her hands she was grasping a third paper with four Xs in a diagonal line. At the bottom of her paper she'd written: *I notice that is the same on both sides*

FIGURE 16-3 Richard was the only student to mark four points on one of the axes. He correctly identified the coordinates for each.

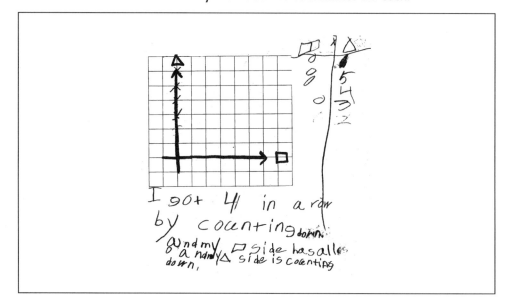

because I am going digle. (See Figure 16–4.) I smiled and assured her that she'd have a chance to share her paper soon. I made a note to myself to remember to experiment with different types of diagonal lines the next day. We would begin with Amy's paper.

Figure 16–5 shows another student's graph.

Amy was excited to discover the pattern of the coordinates in her diagonal pattern of Xs. It was important to follow up her experience so that she saw that a diagonal pattern didn't always produce the same numbers in each pair. For example, a similar diagonal pattern will also result from plotting (3, 2), (4, 3), (5, 4), and (6, 5).

As did Latasha, Marie marked four points vertically and described the patterns in the coordinates. She also added two extra points and recorded their coordinates.

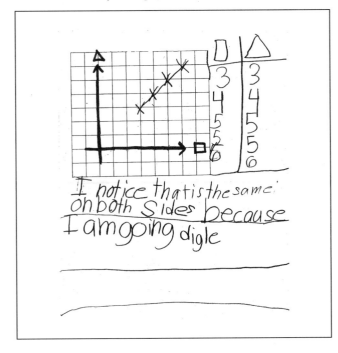

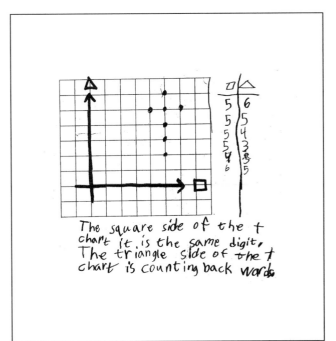

Extensions

On another day, repeat the activity with points on the diagonal. First do an example with the whole class. Mark four points on a diagonal on a blank grid and then have the students help you record on a T-chart. Discuss the patterns. Repeat for four more points on the diagonal, but in the opposite direction. Then explain the class assignment, asking children to win with four points in a diagonal row. As they did before, have them mark the points on a blank game grid, then record the numbers on a T-chart, and finally write about what they notice.

Mathematical Background

It's important to understand the math behind the math you teach. We recognize that some elementary teachers haven't thought a great deal about algebra since taking a course in high school or college and don't feel comfortable with what they remember about algebra. Therefore, what follows are descriptions of a few ideas that are key to algebraic thinking. These ideas are introduced in the lessons, but not with the formal language that's used in the descriptions that follow. Please keep in mind that this is not information that your students are expected to learn, but background information to enhance your understanding. Also, descriptions of other ideas appear in the "Background" sections of individual lessons. We know how difficult it can be to learn mathematics from reading about it. If the information presented here is new to you, our suggestion is to first try the activities in the lessons, and then read the following descriptions after you've had some firsthand experience.

Patterns and Functions

(**Note:** Reading Chapters 1, 3, and 10 first will provide you with a context for the information in this section.)

Patterns provide us with a way to recognize order and make sense of the world. The ability to create, recognize, and extend patterns is essential for making generalizations, seeing relationships, and understanding the order and logic of mathematics. The lessons in this book engage students in investigating both numerical and geometric patterns, building on what they have previously learned.

Students' observations of patterns that define how quantities relate to one another give them beginning experiences with functions. For example, we can look at the pattern of tricycles and wheels—one tricycle has three wheels, two tricycles have six wheels, three have nine wheels, and so on. To find the number of wheels for any number of tricycles, we multiply the number of tricycles by three. The pattern holds for any number of tricycles, and the relationship between these two quantities—the number of tricycles and the number of wheels—is called a *function*. We can represent a function symbolically in several ways. One way is to make a table that's commonly called a T-chart.

tricycles	wheels
0	0
1	3
2	6
3	9
4	12
.	.
.	.
.	.

We can also represent a function as an equation, using symbols for the changing quantities. In this case, one symbol would represent the number of tricycles and another would represent the number of wheels. We can use letters for symbols. For example, if we use t to represent the number of tricycles and w to represent the number of wheels, then we can represent the functional relationship of wheels to tricycles as $w = t \times 3$ or $t \times 3 = w$. Instead of using letters for the symbols, we can use shapes in which we can write numbers; for example, we can draw a box to represent the number of tricycles and a triangle to represent the number of wheels: $\triangle = \square \times 3$.

A third way to represent a function is to make a graph. Using the pairs of numbers from the T-chart as ordered pairs and plotting the points they represent produces the following graph:

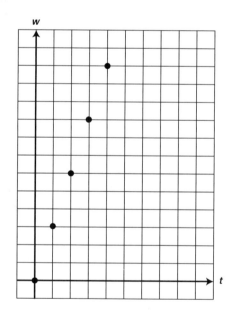

It's also possible to describe a function verbally. For example: *Tricycles have three wheels, so the number of wheels is equal to three times the number of tricycles.* Generalizing a pattern verbally is usually helpful for then representing it algebraically, numerically, or graphically.

More formally, a function is a relationship between two variables in which the value of one variable, often called the *output*, depends on the value of the other, often called the *input*. An important characteristic of a function is that for every input, there is exactly one output. For example, if the rule for a function is to add two to the input number, and an input number is six, then eight is the only possible output number for that input. Using a triangle and a box as symbols to represent the variables, an equation to describe this function rule could be $\triangle = \square + 2$. For every function presented in these lessons, it's possible for students to describe the pattern and identify a rule for determining the output value for any input value. However, that isn't an appropriate focus for K–2 children, and the lessons in this book focus instead on having them explore, extend, and discuss relationships between two quantities.

Variables

(**Note:** Reading Chapter 15 will give you an example of incorporating variables into a lesson for K–2 students.)

Variables are letters, symbols, or other placeholders in mathematical expressions that can serve different purposes. They can represent an unknown value; for example, to make the equation $4x = 12$ true, x must represent the number 3. Variables can also represent the input and output values of a pattern that can be described as a function rule; for example, in $w = t \times 3$, the equation used to describe the function about tricycles and wheels, the letters w and t are variables, while 3 is a constant. Variables can represent quantities in formulas; for example, the A, l, and w in $A = l \times w$ are variables. They can be used to represent a generalized numerical property; for example, in $\square + \triangle = \triangle + \square$, $\square$ and $\triangle$ are variables used to describe the commutative property of addition.

We haven't incorporated variables into most of the lessons in the book but rather have focused on building a foundation of understanding of patterns and relationships that students will later describe algebraically with symbols. For example, in Chapter 1, "Caterpillars," the children discover that the number of circles used to draw a caterpillar is equal to the number of years old the caterpillar is, plus two. In later grades, they will learn to describe a pattern like this algebraically using variables for years and circles; for example: $y + 2 = c$ or $\triangle = \square + 2$.

Graphing Functions

(**Note:** Reading Chapters 5 and 15 will give you an introduction to plotting points and graphing.)

Most of the graphs in the lessons represent linear functions, which means that if you graph them, the points on the graphs lie on a straight line. (For a helpful way to remember this term, notice that the word *line* is contained in *linear*.) Also, most of the lines in the graphs go on a diagonal up to the right. The slant of the diagonal is referred to as the *slope* of the line, and the steeper the line, the higher the slope. The slope is different for the three graphs shown on pages 236–237.

To figure the value of the slope of a line on a graph, examine a sequence of points that have been plotted with the input values in order—0, 1, 2, 3, 4, and so on. Start with any point, count one space to the right, and then see how many spaces you have to count up to reach the next point.

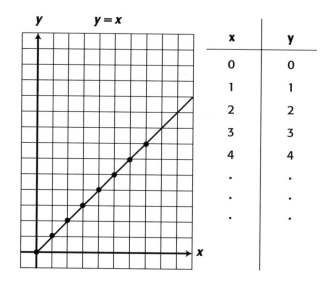

x	y
0	0
1	1
2	2
3	3
4	4
.	.
.	.
.	.

For example, in the first graph (above), to get from one point to the next, each time you count one to the right, you have to count up one to reach the next point. Therefore, the slope of the line on the first graph is 1. In the second graph (below), to get from one point to the next you count up two spaces each time you go over one; therefore, the slope of the second line is 2.

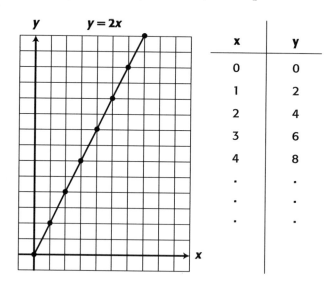

x	y
0	0
1	2
2	4
3	6
4	8
.	.
.	.
.	.

And, in the third graph (see opposite), the slope is 3 because each time you go from one point to the next, you count over one and then up three. The larger the slope, the steeper the line is. For a line that is less steep than the line on the first graph, the slope has to be less than 1. For example, for a line to have a slope of $\frac{1}{2}$, each time you count over one space from a point you would only have to go up half a space to get to the next point.

The value of the slope of a line is evident in the numerical information on the T-chart by examining the pattern of the output values when the inputs are listed in order—0, 1, 2, 3, 4, and so on. For the first graph shown above, the output numbers increase by the same value of 1 each time; in the second graph shown above, they increase by 2; in the third graph shown below, they increase by 3. When the increase of successive output values is a constant, as it is on the T-charts for each of these graphs, the increase is the slope. If the increase in the output values on a T-chart isn't constant, but changes, that indicates that graphing the ordered pairs won't produce points in a straight line but, instead, on a curve. However, for this introductory experience, the points on all of the graphs the students investigate go in straight lines and the graphs are, therefore, linear.

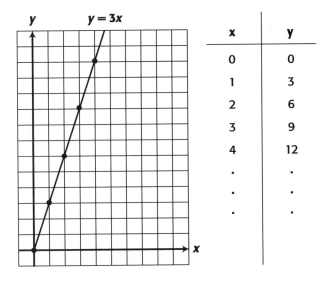

x	y
0	0
1	3
2	6
3	9
4	12
.	.
.	.
.	.

The patterns of the points in graphs connect to the algebraic equations that represent the patterns. Notice that the slope for the graphs on the previous page is the same number that is multiplied by the input variable in the equation. For example, the second graph on page 236 has an equation of $y = 2x$, or $\triangle = 2 \times \square$, and the slope is 2. For a slope of 1, shown in the first graph on page 236, the multiplication isn't indicated in the equation, since multiplying by 1 doesn't change the value of a number. However, we could write the equation as $y = x$, $y = 1 \times x$, or $\triangle = 1 \times \square$.

The previous graphs each show a line that passes through the origin of the coordinate grid. That's because the ordered pair (0, 0) fits each pattern. This isn't always true. For example, if the rule for a pattern is that the output value is equal to two times the input value plus one, the equation would be $y = 2x + 1$, or $\triangle = 2 \times \square + 1$. (You could check the pattern in the output values on a T-chart and the pattern of successive points on the graph to verify that the slope of this graph is 2.) For this particular pattern, if the input value of 0 produces 1, that means that the ordered pair for the input value of 0 is (0, 1). If you graph the pairs of numbers for the T-chart, the line would not go through the origin—it would cross the vertical axis at one space above the origin. The "+ 1" in the rule tells that the line will intercept the vertical axis at one space above the origin.

For the graphs shown earlier, there is no "plus" number in the rule or in the equation. If we wanted to have a "plus" number and still have the same equation, we would have to use "+ 0" in each equation so that the values of the output numbers would stay the same. So, for example, the equation for the second graph on page 236 could be written as $y = 2x + 0$ or $\triangle = 2 \times \square + 0$, and the 0 would indicate where on the vertical axis the line would hit, which is the origin.

If you're not familiar with this aspect of mathematics, investigate the graphs for other equations and see if you can figure out how to predict for any linear equation what the slope of the line will be and where the line will intercept the vertical axis. While this knowledge isn't a goal for the lessons in this book, it's helpful background information for teaching the lessons effectively.

More About Linear Functions

(**Note:** The following information extends the previous information about linear functions and offers you background information beyond the mathematics presented in the lessons.)

It's valuable to look for connections among ideas in mathematics. Making connections strengthens understanding and helps us see mathematics in a cohesive way. In this light, it's helpful to think about connections among the three representations for a function—a T-chart, an equation using variables, and a graph.

In the previous section, "Graphing Functions," connections were made between the equation and the graph that represent a function. One connection is that the slope of the line on a graph is the same as the number that is multiplied by the input variable in the equation. Another connection is that the point where the line intercepts the vertical axis on the graph is the number that is added in the equation. For example, one rule that is presented in Chapter 13 is that the number that comes out of the machine is always equal to three more than the number that is put into the machine. The number put into the machine is the input value; the number that comes out is the output value. For an input of 2, for example, the machine adds 3, producing an output value of 5. For an input of 7, adding 3 produces an output value of 10. Algebraically, using y for the output value and x for the input value, the function rule can be written as $y = x + 3$. The number added in the equation is 3; on the graph, the diagonal line of points intercepts the vertical axis at (0, 3), three above the origin.

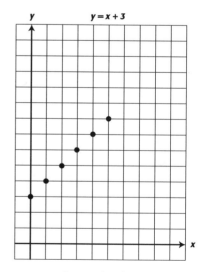

Also, when you go over to the right from one point to the next on the graph, you count up one to reach the next point; that's because the multiplier of x in the equation is 1 (remember that x is the same as 1 times x). This means that the slope of the graph is 1. This information about the equation and the graph also connects to the numerical information on a T-chart. The following is the T-chart for this rule:

x	y
0	3
1	4
2	5
3	6
4	7
5	8
.	.
.	.
.	.

Notice that the difference between the output numbers on the T-chart is 1. This is the multiplier of the input number in the equation (which in this case is 1), and it's also the slope of the graph. Also notice that the output value for the input of 0 is 3. This relates to the number added in the equation and also to where the line crosses the vertical axis on the graph.

When you understand these connections, if you see the T-chart or the equation of a function you'll be able to visualize its graph. Also, if you see a graph, you'll be able to write the equation and create the T-chart. And if you see only the equation, you'll be able to construct the T-chart and make a graph. They're all connected.

In high school algebra books, you'll often see a general equation for linear functions written as $y = mx + b$. In our rule above, $y = x + 3$, $m = 1$, and $b = 3$. There is nothing magical about the choice of m and b in the general equation; they're arbitrary choices for letters that have become one of the symbolic conventions of mathematics. What's important to know is that on a graph of a function, m represents the slope and b represents where the line crosses the vertical axis. Also, on a T-chart representing the function, m is the difference between numbers in the output column and b is the output value when 0 is the input value. A part of understanding mathematics is bringing meaning to the symbols we use to represent ideas.

Blackline Masters

Comparing Handfuls

From *Lessons for Algebraic Thinking, Grades K–2* by Leyani von Rotz and Marilyn Burns. © 2002 Math Solutions Publications.

Tic-Tac-Toe Grid

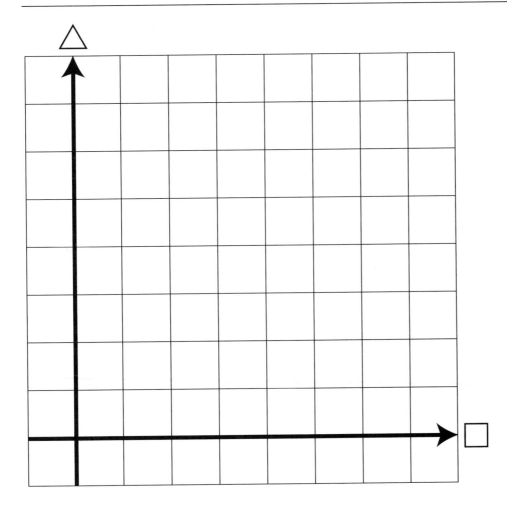

0–99 Chart

0	1	2	3	4	5	6	7	8	9
10	11	12	13	14	15	16	17	18	19
20	21	22	23	24	25	26	27	28	29
30	31	32	33	34	35	36	37	38	39
40	41	42	43	44	45	46	47	48	49
50	51	52	53	54	55	56	57	58	59
60	61	62	63	64	65	66	67	68	69
70	71	72	73	74	75	76	77	78	79
80	81	82	83	84	85	86	87	88	89
90	91	92	93	94	95	96	97	98	99

Two Handfuls

From *Lessons for Algebraic Thinking, Grades K–2* by Leyani von Rotz and Marilyn Burns. © 2002 Math Solutions Publications.

Missing Numbers #1

$$3 + 5 = 4 + $$

$$4 + 1 = + 5$$

$$6 + = 5 + 2$$